Dance In The Vampire Bund

The Memories of Sledgehammer

3

VOLUME

Tamaki Nozomu

SEVEN SEAS ENTERTAINMENT PRESENTS

DANCE IN THE VAMPIRE BUND

The Memories of Sledgehammer

story and art by NOZOMU TAMAKI

VOLUME 3

TRANSLATION
Adrienne Beck

ADAPTATION
Janet Houck

LETTERING
Roland Amago

LAYOUT
Bambi Eloriaga-Amago

COVER DESIGN
Nicky Lim

PROOFREADER
Shanti Whitesides

MANAGING EDITOR
Adam Arnold

PUBLISHER
Jason DeAngelis

DANCE IN THE VAMPIRE BUND:
THE MEMORIES OF SLEDGEHAMMER VOLUME 3

Edited by MEDIA FACTORY.
First published in Japan in 2013 by KADOKAWA CORPORATION, Tokyo.
English translation rights reserved by Seven Seas Entertainment, LLC.
under the license from KADOKAWA CORPORATION, Tokyo.

ISBN: 978-1-626920-69-9
Printed in Canada
First Printing: September 2014
10 9 8 7 6 5 4 3 2 1

READING DIRECTIONS

This book reads from ***right to left***, Japanese style. If this is your first time reading manga, you start reading from the top right panel on each page and take it from there. If you get lost, just follow the numbered diagram here. It may seem backwards at first, but you'll get the hang of it! Have fun!!

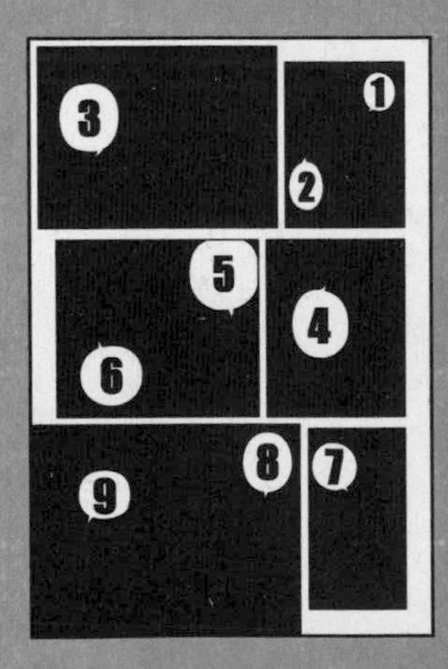

NOK
NOK
HEY!
KCHAK
SO YOU'RE THE ONE LOOKING FOR A BITE, EH?
FOLLOW ME.
THERE'S BEEN A LOT FEWER OF 'EM LATELY, TRYIN' TO SMUGGLE THEIR WAY ONTO THE ISLAND.
ANYBODY WHO WANTED TO BE ONE HAD A... *REAL EASY* WAY JUST A LITTLE WHILE AGO, Y'KNOW.
OUR BUSINESS HAS JUST ABOUT DRIED UP NOW.
SO YOU MISSED OUT ON THAT WHOLE PANDEMIC THING, EH?
BIP
BIP
NO OFFENSE, BUT YOU HAD TO HAVE BEEN PRETTY DAMN SLOW...
PSHUUU

WHA ...?
Y-YOU ...!!
SLCH
Chapter 9: The Callous City

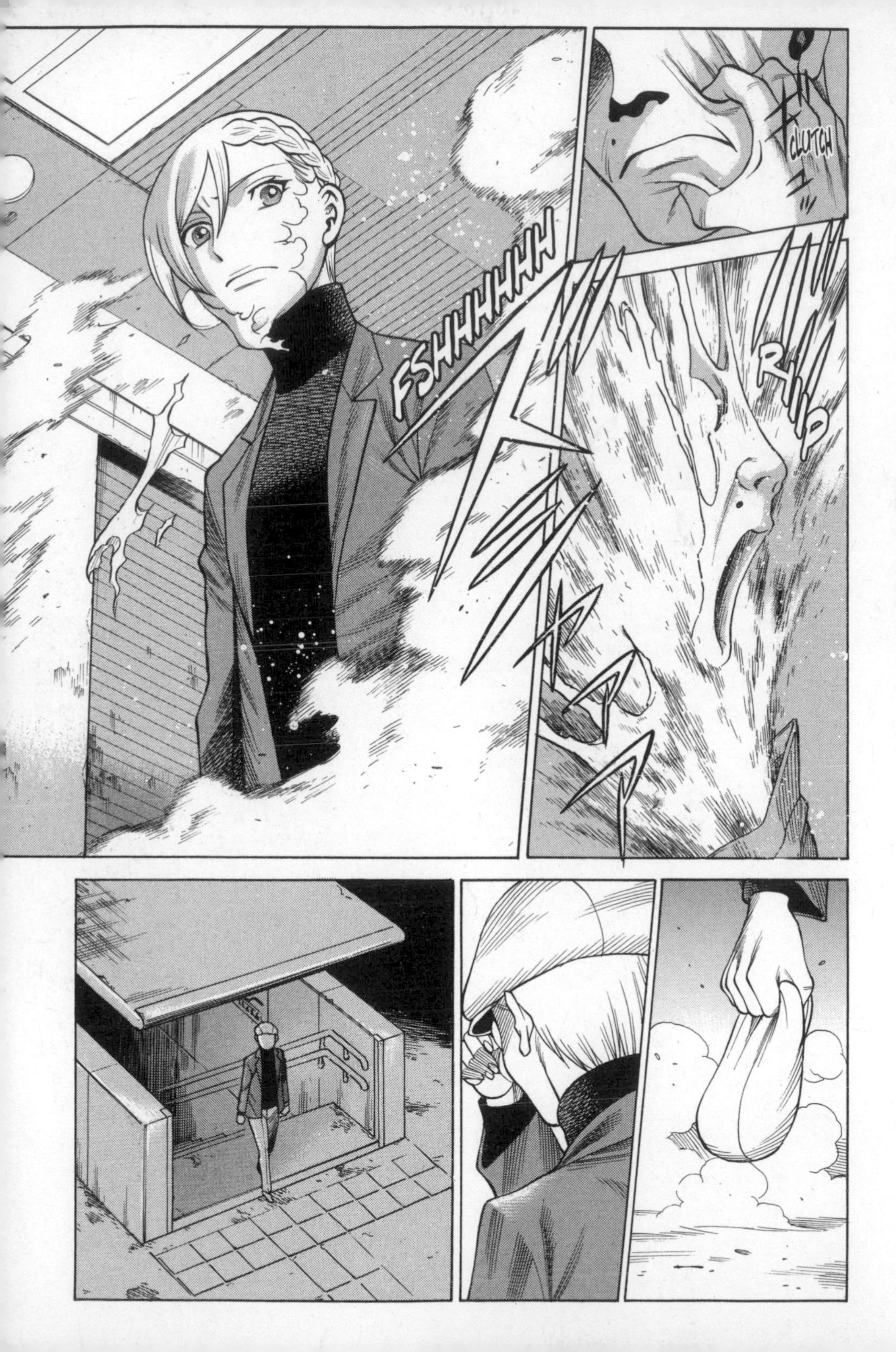
CLUTCH
FSHHHHHH
RIIIP

LORD IN HEAVEN...

ALL OF THESE PEOPLE...
IS EVERY ONE OF THEM A VAMPIRE?
I MUST STAY INCON-SPICIOUS.
IF THEY FIND OUT I'M HUMAN, I'LL HAVE TROUBLE ENOUGH STAYING ALIVE, LET ALONE COMPLETING MY MISSION.
PROCEED TO THE LOCATION MARKED ON THE MAP. ONCE THERE, DIAL THIS NUMBER...
AND YOU WILL BE GIVEN FURTHER INSTRUC-TIONS.

MIDDLE-LEVEL TERRACE, APARTMENT 360.
I HAVE TO HURRY.

VROOM

RIGHT! APARTMENT 360!!
WE FOUND A MAP WITH THAT ADDRESS MARKED IN THE DATA THEY LEFT BEHIND!
THE TARGET HAS PROBABLY ALREADY MANAGED TO SUCCESSFULLY INFILTRATE THE BUND!
UNDERSTOOD!
BOTH THE VGS AND BEOWULF ARE ALREADY EN ROUTE TO THAT LOCATION!

HOWEVER, THE QUESTION IS HOW THAT AGENT PLANNED TO INFILTRATE *THIS BUILDING!*
IF THEIR TARGET IS GOTOH, SHE IS ALREADY ENSCONCED HERE, SURROUNDED BY TOP-LEVEL GOVERNMENT SECURITY!

NO CLUE.
IT WASN'T IN THE INFO WE FOUND.
SKREEE

SO WE'RE GONNA CATCH HER AND ASK HER DIRECTLY!!

maestro
TK
TK
TK

RRING
MASTER, IT'S CLARISSA.
RRING
SO SHE FOLLOWED ORDERS AND HAS ARRIVED AT THE SPECIFIED LOCATION? EXCELLENT.

DECLINE IT.
DO NOT ANSWER ANY FURTHER CALLS SHE MAY MAKE.
PLIP

BEEEEP
!!

IT WAS DROP-PED ...?
BLIP
BLIP
BLIP
WE'RE SORRY. THE PERSON YOU ARE TRYING TO REACH IS NOT ACCEPTING CALLS AT THIS TIME...
WHAT IS GOING ON...?

!
SKREEECH!
ALPHA SQUAD, SECURE THE PERIMETER! EVERYONE ELSE, SEARCH THE BUILDING!!
V.G.S

RRGH!
BIP
BIP
BIP
THE PERSON YOU ARE TRYING TO REACH IS NOT...
DAMN IT! WHAT IS HAPPENING?!
WHOA... HEY, HEY, HEEEY!!

I CAN HARDLY BELIEVE MY EYES, BABE!
LIKE, TOTALLY!!
THERE'S A HUMAN OVER THERE, STANDING SMACK-DAB IN THE MIDDLE OF THE BUND!
C'MERE A SEC, LITTLE GIRL.
OH, DON'T YOU WORRY. WE'RE ONLY GONNA NIBBLE JUST A LITTLE.
HA HA HA HA HA!!

TROMP
TROMP
TROMP
THIS IS ALPHA SQUAD. NO SIGN OF INTRUDERS AROUND THE PERI-METER.
WE WILL STATION LOOKOUTS. THE REMAINDER WILL JOIN THE BUILDING SEARCH.

WAIT A SEC...
HEY!!

*First seen in Dance in the Vampire Bund Vol. 3.

BOOOOOOM
AKIRA!!
TMP
SKSH
WOOSH

WSH
FREEZE! COME BACK HERE!!
AKIRA, YOU OKAY ?!
YEAH! I'M IN PURSUIT OF THE TARGET!
TRY TO GET AHEAD AND CUT HER OFF!
THE INTRUDER IS CURRENTLY MOVING FROM THE RESIDENTIAL DISTRICT'S LUGOSI STREET TOWARDS PRICE AVENUE IN THE COMMERCIAL DISTRICT.
ALL VGS AND BEOWULF PERSONNEL IN THE AREA, PROCEED TO CAPTURE THE TARGET ALIVE.

IT SEEMS CLARISSA HAS BEGUN TO RUN, MASTER.

EXCELLENT. THEN IT IS TIME WE MADE OUR MOVE AS WELL.
WSH

HUP
WHAP
SWOOSH
WHUK

TROMP
TROMP
THUK
THUK
PSHU
BOOM

WHAP
SWIP
NO ENTRY
KRASH
HUP

BAM
DAMMIT!!
KRISH
PLINK
KLAT-TER

GULP...

DWAAAAH?!
THUD
KRISH
AAUGH?!
KRUNCH
KRAAAASH

WHUMP
BRAP
AP
AP
WOOOOSH

KLOOONG
THUD
......
NO WAY...!
THIS IS BRAVO TEAM.
WE ARE CURRENTLY IN PURSUIT OF THE TARGET, MOVING SOUTH DOWN PRICE AVENUE.

THAT'S OUR TARGET? HOO BOY, LOOKIT HER JUMP AND FLY AROUND!
YOU SURE SHE'S HUMAN?!
'CUZ I ALMOST WANNA SCOUT HER FOR BEOWULF!!

!
TROMP

WHERE THE HELL DID ALL THESE PEOPLE COME FROM?!
OUT OF THE WAY! CLEAR THE ROAD!!

THIS IS DELTA TEAM! WE CAN'T MOVE!!
WHISKEY TEAM, HERE! WE'RE IN THE SAME BOAT! SOMEBODY DO SOMETHING ABOUT THIS CROWD!!

HOLY SHIT...! IT'S LIKE THE ENTIRE BUND IS AFTER THAT CHICK!!

......

"LOOKS LIKE THEY LEFT IN A HURRY, THOUGH."
"THE WHOLE ROOM WAS VIRTUALLY UNTOUCHED."
"WOULDN'T THAT BE WAY TOO OBVIOUS?"
INRI

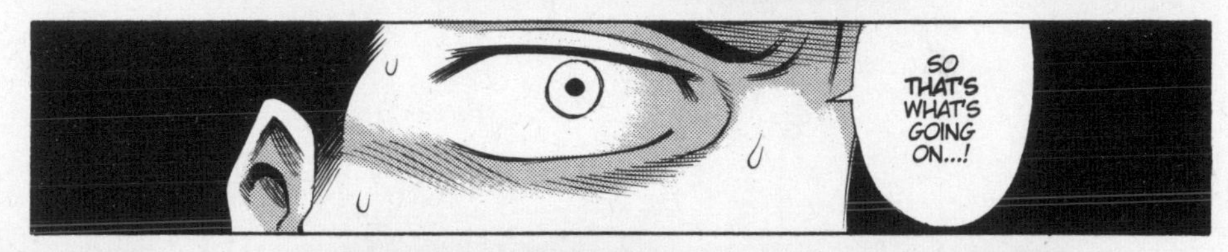
SO THAT'S WHAT'S GOING ON...!

INSPECTOR HAMA?
CALL EVERYBODY BACK!!
SHE'S NOT OUR REAL TARGET!
WHERE ARE YOU GOING?

TO THE GOVERNMENT BUILDING!!

YOU GAVE UP AN ELITE POSITION WITH THE MINISTRY OF FOREIGN AFFAIRS JUST SO YOU COULD FOLLOW REIKO?
OH MY GOSH, HOW ROMANTIC!! ♡
NAAAH, IT WASN'T THAT BIG A DEAL. I JUST WORKED AS A GLORIFIED PAGE.
BESIDES, I COULD HARDLY CALL MYSELF A MAN IF I JUST STOOD BY AND WATCHED A LADY LIKE GOTOH-SAN WALK OUT INTO THE WIDE WORLD, ALL BY HERSELF!

THAT IS *SOOO AMAZING!* FUJIMI, YOU'RE AWESOME!
AWW, IT'S NOT THAT BIG OF A DEAL, MISS.
THEY'RE HAVING FUN.
IT LOOKS LIKE FUJIMI AND MISS ELIE ARE GETTING ALONG REALLY WELL.
WELL, YES. THEY ARE OF A SIMILAR AGE... **MENTALLY.**

NOW THEN, HASEGAWA AND I WILL BE OFF TO PARTY HEADQUARTERS.
WILL YOU BE ALL RIGHT ALONE? ARE YOU SURE YOU DON'T WANT A GUARD?

WE'LL BE FINE, MA'AM. THERE'S ACTUALLY A HIDDEN PASSAGEWAY THAT RUNS UNDERGROUND ALL THE WAY TO THE MAINLAND. IT'S USUALLY FOR USE ONLY BY THE BUND'S INTELLIGENCE AGENTS...
BUT HER MAJESTY HAS GIVEN US SPECIAL PERMISSION TO USE IT THIS ONCE.
THIS WAY, WE WON'T HAVE TO WORRY ABOUT BEING TAILED.

AHA! I KNEW THEY HAD SOMETHING LIKE THAT HIDDEN AROUND HERE!!
YES. THEY HAVE UPLOADED OUR HANDPRINTS INTO THEIR DATABASE AND GIVEN US ACCESS.
MINE, TOO?
NO, JUST THE THREE OF US. WE CAN'T HAVE YOU DECIDING TO TAKE OFF ON YOUR OWN.
WE'LL BE GOING, THEN ...
HASEGAWA !

PARDON ME, MA'AM.
YES, WHAT IS IT?
HER MAJESTY REQUESTS THAT YOU DO NOT LEAVE THIS ROOM FOR THE TIME BEING, MA'AM.
G.S

IS THERE A PROBLEM ?
DO NOT WORRY, MA'AM. THERE IS NO WAY AN INTRUDER COULD INFILTRATE THIS BUILDING.
JUST IN CASE, PLEASE ALLOW US TO MOVE INTO YOUR ROOMS, AS WELL.

LEAVE IT TO ME, GOTOH-SAN!
I'LL PROTECT YOU AND MISS ELIE WITH MY LIFE!

EEE! YOU'RE SO COOL, FUJIMI!
YOU *HAVE* TO COME VISIT MY COUNTRY SOMEDAY! THE GIRLS WON'T BE ABLE TO LEAVE YOU ALONE!!

NAH. I'M REAL FLATTERED, MISS ELIE, BUT I'VE GOTTA STAY LOYAL TO GOTOH-SAN!
OH! RIGHT, RIGHT! I'M SO SORRY!
......

PLEASE COME IN.

HAMA? IT IS ME. WHERE ARE YOU?
ON MY WAY TO YOU, YOUR MAJESTY. THE CROWDS GOT SO BAD, WE HAD TO GIVE UP THE TRUCKS!!
IT'LL STILL BE A FEW MINUTES BEFORE WE'RE THERE!
I HAVE INCREASED THE GUARDS AROUND GOTOH AND THE GUEST CONTINGENT. IS IT TRUE THERE IS ANOTHER ENEMY UNIT IN OPERATION?

THE LAPTOP THAT WAS LEFT OUT IN PLAIN SIGHT.
THE PASSWORD THAT WAS TOO EASY TO GUESS.
I SHOULD'VE REALIZED IT SOONER...
THOSE WERE ALL BAIT! THEY WERE **DELIBERATELY** LEFT OUT WHERE WE COULD FIND THEM!

THE GIRL IS A DECOY!
THE REAL ATTEMPT IS COMING FROM ANOTHER DIRECTION ENTIRELY!!
KCHAK
GOTOH-SAN IS IN TROUBLE! YOU HAVE TO HURRY!
WHAT HAP-PENED?!

THUD
PSHUUU
BAM
FWAP
KRUNCH

KCHAK
GOTOH-SAN! MISS ELIE! RUN!!
SEÑOR BOLTON! SOME-THING'S HAPPEN-ING OUT THERE!
OUR GUARDS WERE JUST--
CHIK

I AM FINISHED PLAYING BABY-SITTER FOR YOU.
BTAM
FROM THIS MOMENT ON, YOU WILL OBEY MY EVERY WORD.
SEÑOR ...
BOLTON ...?
CHK
AAH, SO THIS IS IT.
IT IS FINALLY MINE...
THE EDELMAN REPORT!
?!

DON'T YOU DARE PUT YOUR DIRTY HANDS ...
ON GOTOH-SAN!!
BLAM
SPLUK
SPLUK
BLAM
SPLT
NGUH ...!
SPLT
AGH...
FUJIMI-KUN!!
CLUTCH
SLIDE

KYAAAAAAAAA

Chapter 10: Lashou Shentan ~Hard Boiled~

SPLOOSH
BOOM

BLEAH ...
NGK ...!
HAAH ...

WE'RE SORRY. THE PERSON YOU ARE TRYING TO REACH IS NOT ACCEPTING CALLS AT THIS TIME...
maestro
"MAY I ASK WHY WE ARE MAKING THIS TRANSFER IN SUCH AN OPEN AND RISKY MANNER?"
"THERE ARE REASONS WHY THAT IS INAD-VISABLE."
maestro
"IF YOU TRULY BELIEVE SO, TAKE OFF THAT HAT."
"ALL YOU NEED DO IS FOLLOW ORDERS WITHOUT QUESTION."
"IT'S DISRESPECTFUL TO COVER YOUR HEAD IN THE PRESENCE OF THE MASTER'S REPRESENTA-TIVE."
WSH

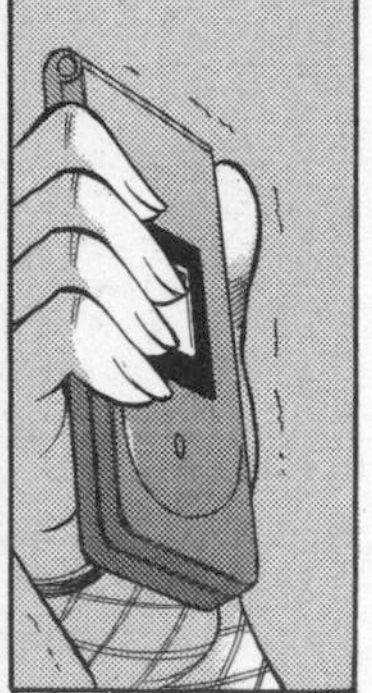

W-
WAIT...
WAIT FOR THE LORD...
SPLOSH
SPLOSH
BE STRONG.

TAKE HEART, AND WAIT...
SPLOSH
SPLOSH
FOR THE LORD.

KREEE
AH ...!

SLIIIDE
スル

TOK

FATHER ... PLEASE ...!

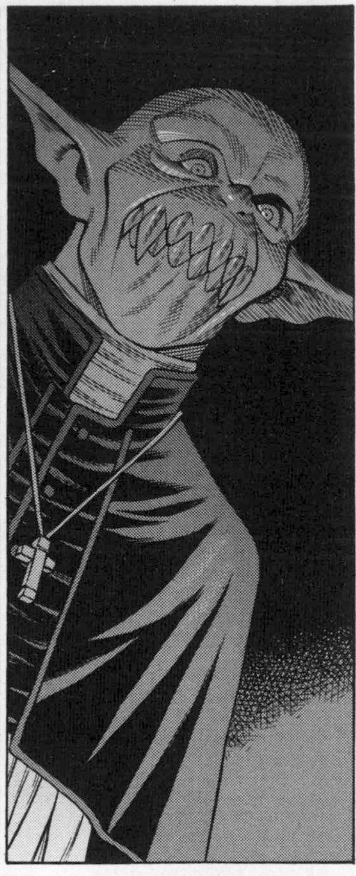

A...
A DEMON ...?

MY APOLOGIES, HAMA.
THEY DUPED US.

THEY USED VISITOR PASSES TO WALK RIGHT IN AND OUT OF THIS BUILDING...
PASSES I GAVE THEM *MYSELF.*

HOW'D THEY GET OFF THE ISLAND?

THE TUNNEL GATES ARE SUPPOSED TO BE SEALED OFF TO **EVERYONE.** NO MATTER WHAT CLEARANCES THEY HAVE, THEY SHOULD HAVE BEEN STOPPED.
SO HOW DID THEY GET OUT?

THEY USED THE INTELLIGENCE DIVISION'S UNDERGROUND PASSAGE.
A VISITOR PASS SHOULDN'T HAVE GOTTEN THEM IN THERE!
NOT EVEN GOTOH-SAN HAS THOSE CLEARANCES.
CORRECT.
BUT HER AIDES DID.

FUJIMI ...
DON'T TELL ME HE HAD A HAND IN THIS!

YES, BUT *NOT* IN THE WAY YOU THINK.

"HAD A HAND" ...?

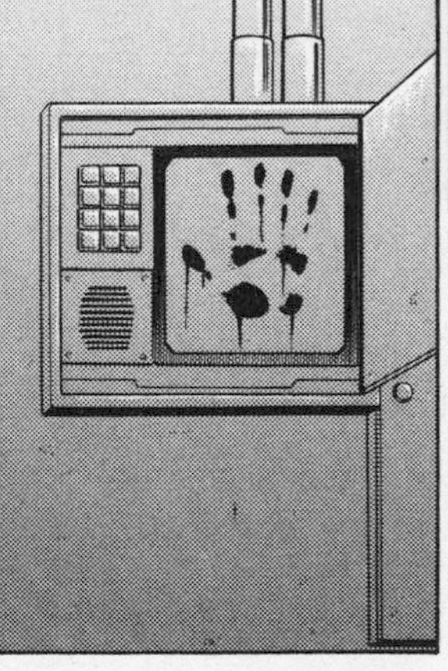

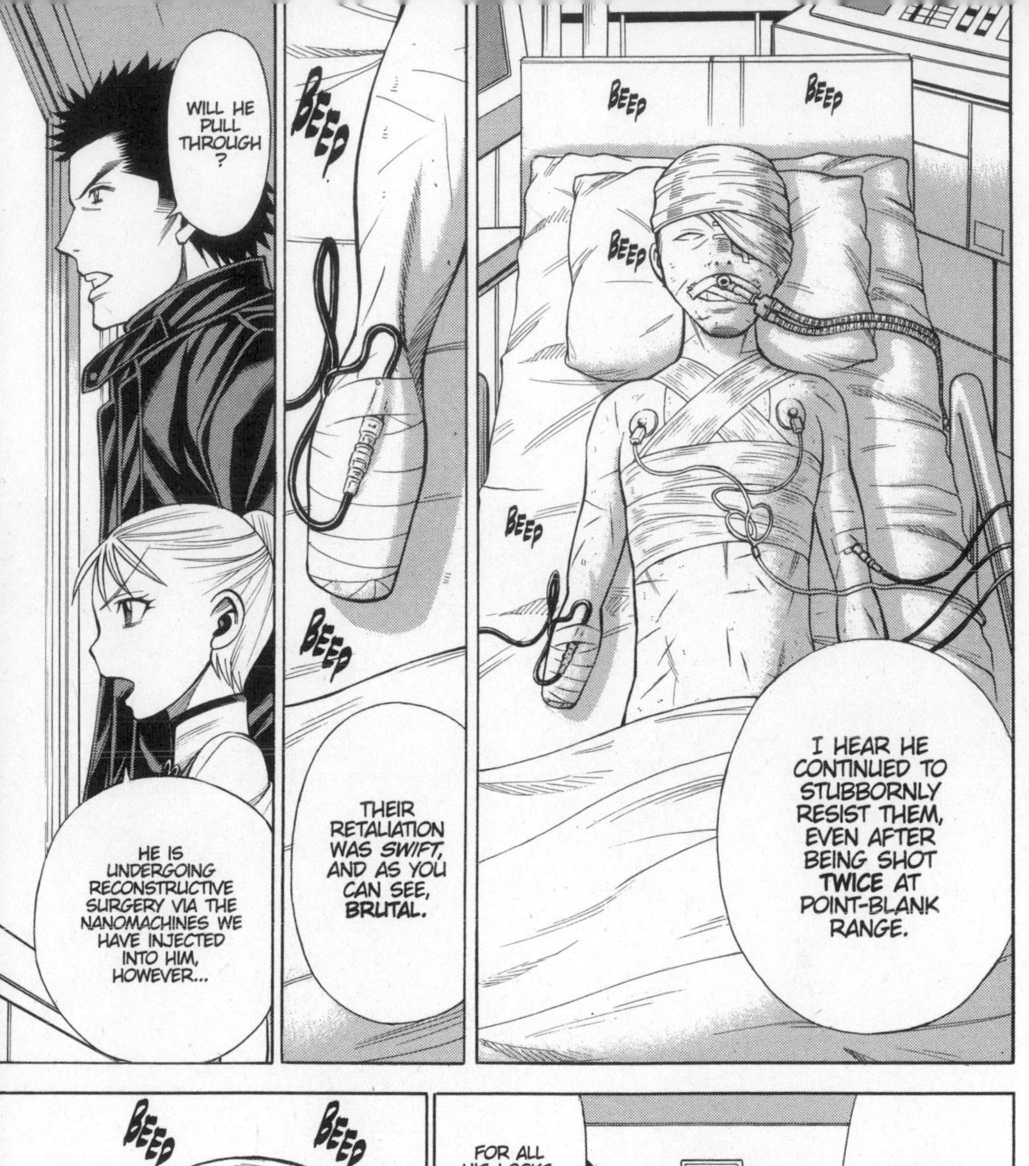
BEEP
BEEP
BEEP
BEEP
I HEAR HE CONTINUED TO STUBBORNLY RESIST THEM, EVEN AFTER BEING SHOT **TWICE** AT POINT-BLANK RANGE.
BEEP
BEEP
THEIR RETALIATION WAS *SWIFT*, AND AS YOU CAN SEE, **BRUTAL.**
WILL HE PULL THROUGH ?
HE IS UNDERGOING RECONSTRUCTIVE SURGERY VIA THE NANOMACHINES WE HAVE INJECTED INTO HIM, HOWEVER...

HE HAS CLUNG TO CONSCIOUSNESS TO THIS POINT BECAUSE HE SAYS THERE IS SOMETHING HE MUST TELL YOU.
FSHUU
FOR ALL HIS LOOKS, HE CERTAINLY HAS A RESPECTABLE DOSE OF COURAGE, MORE THAN YOU'D EXPECT.

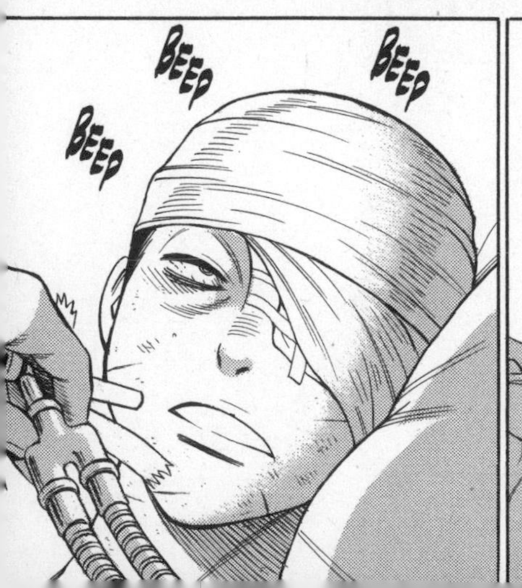
BEEP
BEEP
BEEP

THE PENDANT ...
HE WANTED... GOTOH-SAN'S LUCK CHARM...
TH-THAT'S WHY...
!

SAID SOMETHIN'... 'BOUT "EDELMAN REPORT."
BUT WHO KNOWS WHAT THAT...
THAT TATTOOED BASTARD MEANT... BY THAT.
!
TAT-TOOED ?!
YOU MEAN, BOLTON ?!
SIR, GO EASY ON HIM!
YEAH.
HIM.
RIGHT ON 'IS CHEST...

A BIG OL' TATTOO ...
OF A CROSS.

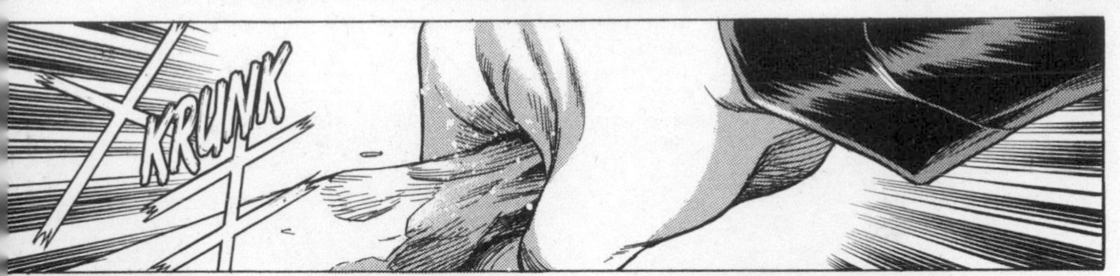
KRUNK

BOLTON!
HE'S THE ONE...!!

HAMA-SAN...
I KEPT... M'PROMISE...

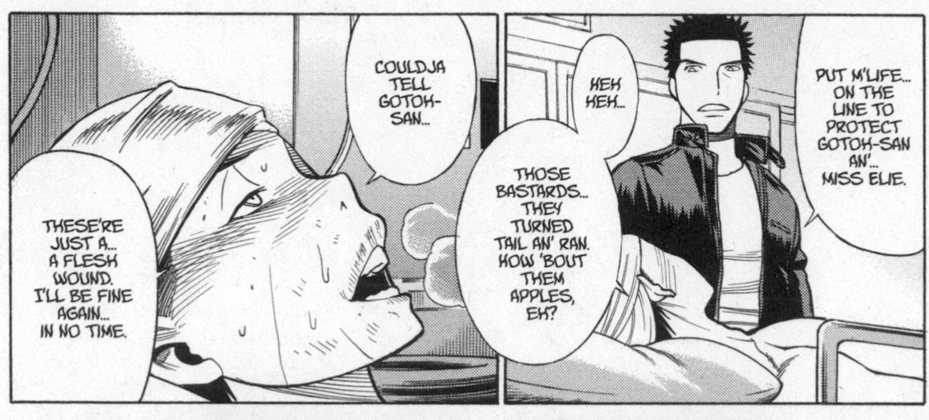
PUT M'LIFE... ON THE LINE TO PROTECT GOTOH-SAN AN'... MISS ELIE.
KEK KEK...
THOSE BASTARDS... THEY TURNED TAIL AN' RAN. HOW 'BOUT THEM APPLES, EH?
COULDJA TELL GOTOH-SAN...
THESE'RE JUST A... A FLESH WOUND. I'LL BE FINE AGAIN... IN NO TIME.

THE TRAUMA FROM HIS INJURIES HAS HIM CONFUSED.
HE THINKS BOTH LADIES WERE SAVED BY HIS SACRIFICE.

GOOD WORK.
I KNEW THERE WAS SOMETHING **SPECIAL** ABOUT YOU.

KEK...
KEK KEK...
YEAH.
I... FINALLY MADE YOU... SAY IT...

BEEEEEE
STAND BACK!
BOTH HEART RATE AND BLOOD PRESSURE ARE DROPPING RAPIDLY!
FSHUU
I HAVE THE INTELLIGENCE DIVISION GOING OVER **EVERY SECOND** OF OUR INTERNAL SECURITY CAMERAS' FOOTAGE, SEARCHING FOR WHERE BOLTON MAY HAVE GONE.
YOU WON'T FIND HIM.
THEY HAVE DETAILED KNOWLEDGE OF OUR SURVEILLANCE SYSTEMS. SO DETAILED THEY WERE EVEN ABLE TO USE IT AGAINST US, TO SET US AFTER THEIR DECOY.
HE WON'T LEAVE ANY CLUES FOR US TO FIND.
SO WE ARE WITH-OUT ANY LEADS...
BAH!
BAM

HAMA-SAN...
RING
RING
INCOMING CALL
Father Diablo
IT'S FROM FATHER DIABLO ...?

PLIP
PLIP

!
FWUMP
ELIE!
ELIE!!
REIKO...
OH THANK GOD! ARE YOU ALL RIGHT?

YES. WHERE ARE WE?
I DON'T KNOW.
IT LOOKS LIKE IT MIGHT BE THEIR HIDEOUT.

KACHUK
!

GET OUT HERE, WOMAN.

SEÑOR BOLTON...!
YOU FILTHY COWARD! YOU USED ME AND MY DADDY, DIDN'T YOU?!
DON'T YOU HAVE ANY SHAME?!

SMAK
WHAT ARE YOU DOING?! LEAVE HER ALONE!!

THAT HARLOT'S FATHER MADE DEALS WITH VAMPIRES, AND EVEN WENT AS FAR AS HELPING TO SAVE THEIR WHORE QUEEN.
HE IS A DESPICABLE HERETIC WHO SPITS ON GOD'S NAME.
AS THE FATHER SINS, SO DOES THE DAUGHTER.
PREPARE YOURSELF.
I WILL DISPENSE THE APPROPRIATE SENTENCE ON YOU MYSELF... LATER.
STRING HER UP.
ELIE!
KACHUK
ELIE!!

KLANG
RATTLE RATTLE
POK
GRIK
NGH!

SO THIS IS A FACTORY ...?

THERE'S NOTHING, SIR. I TOOK IT ALL THE WAY APART...
BUT THERE IS NO SIGN OF ANYTHING CONCEALED INSIDE OF IT.
THEN YOU MUST HAVE TAKEN IT OUT.
WHERE DID YOU HIDE IT?!

TELL ME WHERE YOUR FATHER'S *SECRET REPORT* IS!!
!

MY FATHER'S... *WHAT?*

DON'T PLAY INNOCENT WITH ME! WE ALREADY KNOW THIS PENDANT WAS BEQUEATHED TO YOU BY YOUR DEAD SISTER, NICOLE EDELMAN!
WHAT IS HE TALKING ABOUT? THAT PENDANT WAS ONE OF TWO THAT WERE GIVEN TO ME AND NICOLE...
WHEN FATHER LEFT WITH HER FOR THE UNITED STATES.
!

WE KNOW YOU HAVE SEEN IT!
TELL ME, OR ELSE!!
SO THAT REPORT IS WHAT YOU HAVE BEEN AFTER, NOT ME.
WHY DO YOU WANT IT? WHAT WOULD YOU DO WITH IT?
I AM THE ONE ASKING THE QUES- TIONS!
OKAY, YOU WANT ANSWERS ?! I'LL GIVE YOU ANSWERS !!

I'VE NEVER EVEN HEARD OF THE "EDELMAN REPORT" BEFORE NOW.
IF YOU CAME TO ME LOOKING FOR IT, YOU'RE BARKING UP THE WRONG TREE!
WHAT A TRANS-PARENT LIE!
IT'S THE TRUTH! I LOST ALL CONTACT WITH MY FATHER WHEN I WAS A CHILD. I'VE NEVER SEEN HIM ONCE SINCE THEN! I DIDN'T EVEN GO TO HIS FUNERAL TEN YEARS AGO!!

IT SEEMS YOU ARE UNDERESTIMATING OUR ORGANIZATION'S ABILITIES.
WE HAVE SUCCESSFULLY OVERCOME ALL OF OUR ENEMIES, IN ACCORDANCE WITH GOD'S WILL.

THIS IS A DEVICE THAT WAS USED BY INQUISITORS DURING THE WITCH HUNTS OF THE 17TH CENTURY.
WITH THIS, THEY WERE ABLE TO FLUSH THE HERETICS OUT OF THE STREETS...
AND WRENCH THEIR CONFESSIONS OF GUILT FROM THEM.
TUNK

WOULD YOU LIKE TO KNOW HOW IT WORKS? WE WILL USE YOUR FINGERS, FIRST.
HOLD HER!
STOP!
NO!
WAIT!
I SAID WAIT!!

WHEN DID I SAY I WOULDN'T COOPER-ATE WITH YOU?!
I HAVE NO DESIRE WHATSOEVER TO LOSE MY LIFE, THANKS TO SOMETHING MY DEAD FAMILY DID A DECADE AGO.
AND ESPECIALLY SINCE ELIE'S SAFETY IS RIDING IN THE BALANCE.
TELL ME EVERYTHING YOU KNOW ABOUT THE EDELMAN REPORT.
I MAY BE ABLE TO HELP YOU FIND SOME CLUES.

...
CLUES LIKE WHY MY SISTER MAY HAVE CHOSEN TO SEND THE PENDANT TO ME!
I HAVE TO PRETEND TO GO ALONG WITH THEM...
AND BUY AS MUCH TIME AS I CAN.
EVEN A MINUTE-- NO, EVEN ONE SECOND MORE COULD BE ENOUGH.
IF I CAN JUST HOLD ON LONG ENOUGH...

HAMA-KUN WILL RESCUE US.
I KNOW HE WILL.
KREEE
WELCOME.

NH ...
I HEARD THIS YOUNG LADY'S CONFESSION.
IT SEEMS ONLY YOU CAN GRANT SALVATION FROM THIS TRIAL OF HERS, INSPECTOR.
THIS GIRL IS WANTED AS AN ACCOMPLICE TO A KIDNAPPING. WHY BRING HER TO ME?
THEY SAY EVEN THE LION WILL SPARE THE SUPPLIANT.
IN OTHER WORDS, I'D LIKE TO MAKE AN APPEAL TO YOUR SENSE OF MERCY.

HEH. WHAT A DEVIOUS PRIEST YOU ARE.
YOU DO REALIZE REVEALING A CONFESSION WILL GET YOU EXCOMMUNICATED, RIGHT?

HA HA! OH, I WAS EXCOMMUNICATED A LONG TIME AGO.
THE MOMENT I BECAME LIKE I AM NOW, IN FACT.

MMH ...!

FWUMP

RELAX. THIS IS GOD'S HOUSE.
I WON'T SHED BLOOD HERE.

I'VE GOT SOME QUES-TIONS FOR YOU.
DEPENDING ON HOW YOU ANSWER, I MIGHT EVEN LET YOU WALK.

THERE'S NO REASON FOR YOU TO BE STUBBORN ABOUT THIS, EITHER.
YOUR PLAN WORKED. YOU GOT GOTOH-SAN.
LETTING A FEW DETAILS LEAK WON'T CHANGE THE OVERALL SITUATION.

......

WHAT DO YOU WANT TO KNOW?

WHAT IS THIS "EDELMAN REPORT" YOU GUYS ARE AFTER?

...
JONAS EDELMAN WAS A JOURNALIST.
LEARNING OF THE EXISTENCE OF VAMPIRES AT A YOUNG AGE, HE DEDICATED HIS LIFE TO DISCOVERING THEIR SOCIETY AND HOW IT CONNECTED WITH HUMANITY.

HIS DEDICATION TO THIS CAUSE WAS TREMENDOUS. HE WAS *ENTIRELY OBSESSED.*
AFTER ALL...

THE MOMENT HE DISCOVERED VAMPIRES HAD FORGED A CONNECTION WITH THE JAPANESE GOVERNMENT ...
HE MOVED TO JAPAN, INGRATIATED HIMSELF WITH A FAMILY OF "MEDIATORS," AND EVEN SIRED CHILDREN WITH THE FAMILY'S DAUGHTER.

HIS EXTENSIVE RESEARCH, CONDUCTED AT GREAT PERSONAL COST, CREATED AN INCREDIBLE VOLUME OF PAPERS, BUT NONE OF THESE WERE EVER PUBLISHED.
THIS, OF COURSE, WAS ALL BEFORE MINA TEPES HAD REVEALED HERSELF TO HUMANITY.
WHILST THE EXISTENCE OF VAMPIRES WAS A *PUBLIC SECRET,* THE TRUTH REMAINED BURIED IN THE DARKNESS.

AS, SOON ENOUGH ...
WAS JONAS HIMSELF.
THE OFFICIAL STORY IS THAT HE WAS KILLED IN A CAR ACCIDENT.
POLICE L

BUT HIS LIFE'S WORK WAS TAKEN UP BY HIS DAUGHTER...
A DAUGHTER CAUGHT UP IN THE SAME OBSESSION AS HER FATHER.
!

IT SEEMS NICOLE EDELMAN FAR OUTSTRIPPED HER FATHER AS A JOURNALIST.
SHE BROUGHT A FRESH VIEWPOINT TO HER FATHER'S RESEARCH, DISCOVERING CONNECTIONS HE HAD NEVER SEEN.
SHE INCLUDED **EVERYTHING** IN HER REPORTS... PROOF OF SECRET PACTS BETWEEN VAMPIRES AND NATIONAL LEADERS THROUGHOUT HISTORY.
LISTS OF THE WEALTHY AND POWERFUL, ENSLAVED TO VAMPIRE MASTERS. DETAILED CHARTS ON THE FLOW OF VAMPIRE RESOURCES INTO HUMANITY'S COFFERS.

HOWEVER, SHE TOO LEFT THE WORLD BEFORE SHE HAD A CHANCE TO PUBLISH HER FINDINGS.
そんな時間は
SHE LOST HER LIFE IN A BAFFLING AND *HIGHLY INGLORIOUS* WAY.
YES. *THAT* IS THE EDELMAN REPORT.

AFTER HER DEATH, WE MADE A THOROUGH INVESTIGATION OF ALL SHE HAD LEFT BEHIND, LOOKING FOR CLUES...
WE SPENT MORE TIME ON THAT SEARCH THAN YOU COULD COMPRE-HEND.

THEN THAT'S ...!

IT IS A RECORD, WRITTEN ACROSS TWO GENERA-TIONS...
OF ALL THE WAYS IN WHICH VAMPIRES HAVE RULED OUR WORLD, FROM PAST TO PRESENT!

DURING THAT TIME, I PUT TOGETHER A CERTAIN THEORY.
PERHAPS SHE, LIKE HER FATHER, BEQUEATHED HER FINAL REPORT TO SOMEONE JUST BEFORE HER DEATH.
AND PERHAPS THAT "SOMEONE" WAS HER LAST LIVING RELATIVE.
THAT LOCKET WAS GIVEN TO NICOLE BY HER FATHER.
IT WAS ALSO ONE OF HER FEW BELONGINGS THAT WAS MISSING AFTER HER DEATH.
I GAVE THE ORDER FOR YOUR KIDNAPPING TO MY MEN ALREADY STATIONED IN JAPAN.
WHAT ...?!
UNBE-LIEV-ABLE!
...
NO.
HEH HEH...
THAT WAS QUITE A BOON FOR YOU, YOU KNOW. I HAD ORIGINALLY SENT THEM THERE TO KILL YOU AS A HERETIC WHO HAD SOLD HER SOUL TO VAMPIRES.
THIS IS NOT SOMETHING SOMEONE AS LOWLY AS I COULD DECIDE.
WHEN I SAW THE IMAGE OF WHAT ONE OF MY MEN DISCOVERED IN BATTLE, I KNEW MY THEORY WAS CORRECT.
IT WAS THAT PENDANT.
SHE MUST HAVE HIDDEN SOME SORT OF MEMORY DEVICE IN IT AND SENT IT TO YOU...
SHE MUST HAVE !!

THAT IS ALL I CAN TELL YOU.

NO, THERE'S ONE MORE THING.

YOU CAN TELL ME **WHERE** THEY'RE HIDING.
!

DO YOU THINK I WILL JUST THROW AWAY GOD'S FAVOR AND SELL OUT MY COMRADES ?!
EVEN THOUGH THEY'VE ALREADY SOLD YOU OUT?

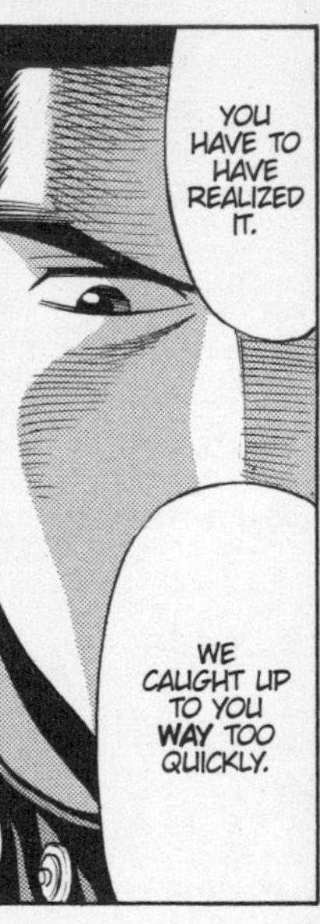
YOU HAVE TO HAVE REALIZED IT.
WE CAUGHT UP TO YOU **WAY** TOO QUICKLY.

WHO ORDERED YOU TO EXPOSE YOUR FACE TO OUR SECURITY CAMERAS?
WHY DO YOU THINK THEY LEFT A LAPTOP WITH THE WHOLE PLAN ON IT, RIGHT WHERE WE COULD FIND IT?
THEY WERE USING YOU AS A THROW-AWAY **DECOY** FROM THE START.

...

'COURSE, I'M NOT EXPECTING YOU TO DO IT FOR FREE.

DANGLE

THERE WERE TWO PENDANTS.

I DOUBT THE OTHER ONE HAS A DAMN THING IN IT.
IF THERE'S ANY SECRET INFORMATION, IT'LL BE IN *THIS* ONE.

YOUR ORGANIZATION'S MISSION IS TO ACQUIRE THE DATA IN HERE, RIGHT?
AND YOU HAVEN'T BEEN FUSSY ABOUT HOW YOU GET IT.
NO REASON TO START GETTING PICKY NOW, ESPECIALLY WHEN YOU STILL NEED A WAY TO GET OUT OF THE BUND ALIVE.

IT'S UP TO YOU.
CHOOSE.
NOW!!

Chapter 11: Better Tomorrow

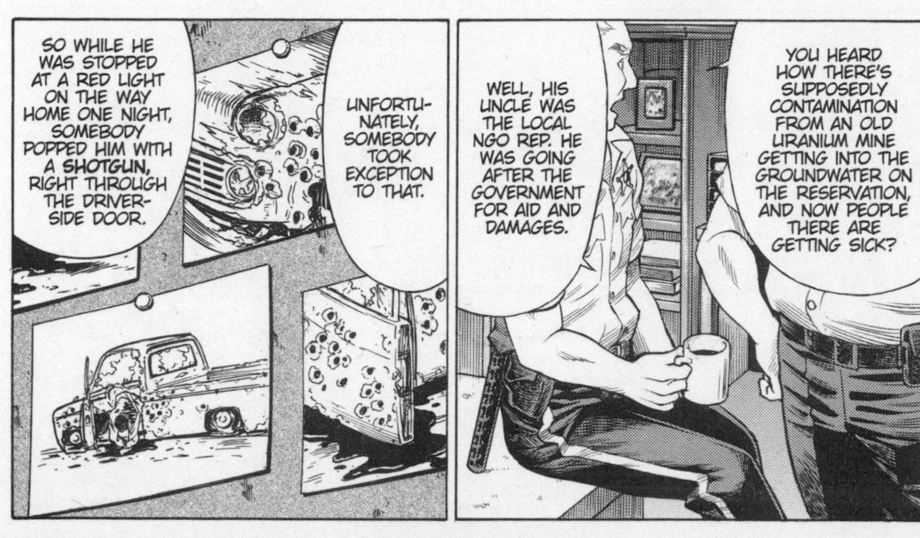
YOU HEARD HOW THERE'S SUPPOSEDLY CONTAMINATION FROM AN OLD URANIUM MINE GETTING INTO THE GROUNDWATER ON THE RESERVATION, AND NOW PEOPLE THERE ARE GETTING SICK?
WELL, HIS UNCLE WAS THE LOCAL NGO REP. HE WAS GOING AFTER THE GOVERNMENT FOR AID AND DAMAGES.
UNFORTU-NATELY, SOMEBODY TOOK EXCEPTION TO THAT.
SO WHILE HE WAS STOPPED AT A RED LIGHT ON THE WAY HOME ONE NIGHT, SOMEBODY POPPED HIM WITH A **SHOTGUN**, RIGHT THROUGH THE DRIVER-SIDE DOOR.

WE ALREADY HAD A LIST OF LIKELY SUSPECTS.
THEY'RE A PACK OF SORRY DRUNKS WHO FANCY THEMSELVES "PATRIOTS"...
NO DOUBT SOMEBODY PAID THEM TO OFF THE GUY.
DIDN'T HAVE ANY CONCLUSIVE PROOF, THOUGH.
SO THE KID THERE WENT AND DISPENSED SOME **JUSTICE** OF HIS OWN.

POOR KID.
HIS DAD WAS A SOLDIER KILLED IN ACTION. HIS MOM, A JAPANESE IMMIGRANT, NEVER DID GET USED TO LIVING ON THE RESERVATION.
SHE COMMITTED SUICIDE WHEN HE WAS TEN YEARS OLD.
HIS UNCLE WAS HIS LAST LIVING RELATIVE. RAISED 'IM LIKE HIS OWN SON.
IT'S NO WONDER THE KID WANTED A LITTLE REVENGE.

SO WHAT'S GOING TO HAPPEN TO HIM NOW?
HIS VICTIMS ALL BEING SCUMBAGS ISN'T ENOUGH TO GET HIM ACQUITTED.
TRUE, TRUE...

KCHAK

YOU'RE SEIJI HAMA?
I'M SERGEANT FIRST-CLASS **GERNSBACK**, THE ARMY RECRUITER FOR THIS DISTRICT.

I HEARD ABOUT WHAT HAPPENED LAST NIGHT.
THAT WAS QUITE THE REPRE-HENSIBLE THING TO DO, SON.

HOWEVER, YOUR CASE DOES HAVE A LOT OF MITIGATING FACTORS.
THE SHERIFF OF THE NAVAJO NATION HIMSELF HAS REQUESTED A *VERY LENIENT* SENTENCE.
SO THE COURT HAS DECIDED TO GIVE YOU A CHANCE.
WHAT YOU DID DISPLAYED A SURPRISING AMOUNT OF ATHLETIC TALENT...
BUT YOU ARE STILL ONLY SEVENTEEN, CORRECT?

SERVE A YEAR OF **PROBATION,** AND ONCE YOU TURN EIGHTEEN, YOU CAN ENLIST IN THE ARMY.
USE THAT EXCEPTIONAL TALENT OF YOURS FOR THE SAKE OF YOUR COUNTRY.

YOU CAN BE A SOLDIER, SON, *OR* BE A CONVICT.
YOU GET TO CHOOSE.

IF I ENLIST...
WILL I GET STRONGER?
?
I'LL DO IT. IT'S NOT LIKE I HAVE ANYWHERE TO GO HOME TO, NOW.

THE YOUNG MAN LOST EVERYTHING... AND THEN LOST EVEN MORE.
NEVER IN HIS YOUNG LIFE DID HE HAVE THE TIME TO DISCOVER WHAT IT WAS HE TRULY WANTED.
BESIDES...
I WAS NEVER REALLY IN A POSITION TO CHOOSE IN THE FIRST PLACE.

CHAK
CHAK
GA-CHOK
THUMP

BA-THUD
NGK ...!
KRAAASH
Mercedes Benz
KLATTER
KLATTER
HFF...
HFF...
HFF...
PSHT

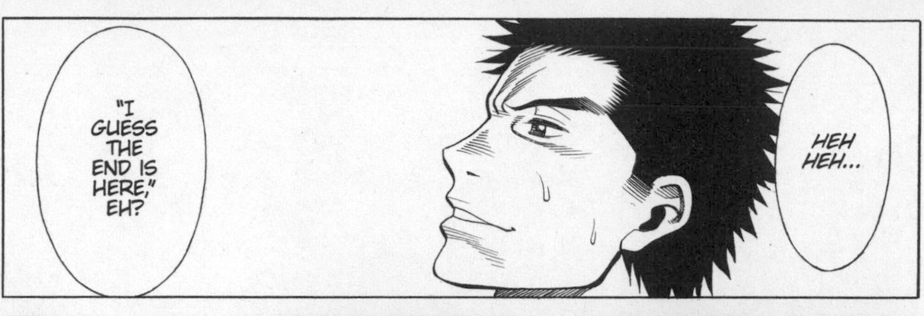
HEH HEH...
"I GUESS THE END IS HERE," EH?

I GUESS THE END IS HERE, HAMMER.

—FOUR YEARS AGO, MINNESOTA, USA.—
THE CURTAIN'S COMING DOWN ON THIS LITTLE HONEYMOON OF OURS.
THE CLAN HAS OFFICIALLY DECIDED TO ABANDON THE ARTIFICIAL BEAST-MAN EXPERIMENTS.

AFTER ALL THE HUNDREDS OF ADJUSTMENTS AND THOUSANDS OF TRIALS, THE ONLY SUBJECT WHO'S STILL CAPABLE OF NORMAL FUNCTION...
HELL, THE ONLY ONE WHO'S STILL EVEN SANE, IS YOU.
YOU REALLY WERE A SPECIAL ONE.
THE CLAN'S PROGRAM TO MASS PRODUCE BEAST-MEN HAS FAILED...
AND OUR TEAM IS BEING DISSOLVED.

SO I'M GETTING KICKED TO THE CURB, HUH?
DO YOU *REALLY* THINK MY LORD WILL TOSS OUT A TOY AS AMUSING AS YOU?
RELAX. LORD ROZENMANN HIMSELF WILL GRANT YOU AN APPROPRIATE PLAYGROUND BEFORE LONG.
UNTIL THEN, GET OUT AND STRETCH YOUR LEGS. YOU'RE OFFICIALLY LIBERATED FROM "GUINEA PIG" STATUS.

WHAT'S GOING TO HAPPEN TO YOU?
WELL, ANY CHANCES I HAD OF PROMOTION ARE SHOT.
BUT DON'T WORRY. THEY AREN'T GOING TO PIN RESPONSIBILITY FOR THIS ON ME AND HAVE ME EXECUTED OR ANYTHING. GENIUS LIKE MINE ISN'T EASY TO FIND.
I MEAN IT. *RELAX.*
NO MATTER WHAT CORNER OF THE EARTH I WASH UP IN, I'LL STILL KEEP MAKING AND SENDING YOU THE SERUM YOU NEED.
I SWEAR ON MY OWN INTELLECT.
I'LL TRUST YOU ON THAT.

GOODBYE, HAMMER... NO, SEIJI.
THE FEW YEARS I SPENT WITH YOU WERE MORE EXCITING AND FULFILLING THAN THE WHOLE CENTURY-PLUS THAT PRECEDED IT.

SO WHAT'RE YOU GONNA DO, OTIS?
I ALREADY TOLD YA, BOSS. I'M STICKING WITH YOU, NO MATTER WHERE YOU GO.

THAT'S NOT WHAT I MEANT.
I ASKED WHAT YOU'RE GONNA DO WITH THIS VACATION TIME WE'VE SUDDENLY GOT.

GOOD POINT. MAN, WHEN WAS THE LAST TIME WE GOT ANY LEAVE?
Y'KNOW, I THINK I WANT SOME BEACH, BOOZE, AND BABES. MAYBE I'LL GO TO **FLORIDA**.
WHAT ABOUT YOU?

ME?
I DUNNO ...

TARGET
TDR
D.Haller. Inc.
tkts
WAY
THE NEW GREEK AND ROMAN GALLERIES
YEEEP!!
HN?
FWAP

OH MY GOSH!
I'M SO SORRY!
REALLY! I'M VERY SORRY ABOUT THIS!
RSTL RSTL
IT'S OKAY ...

SHF

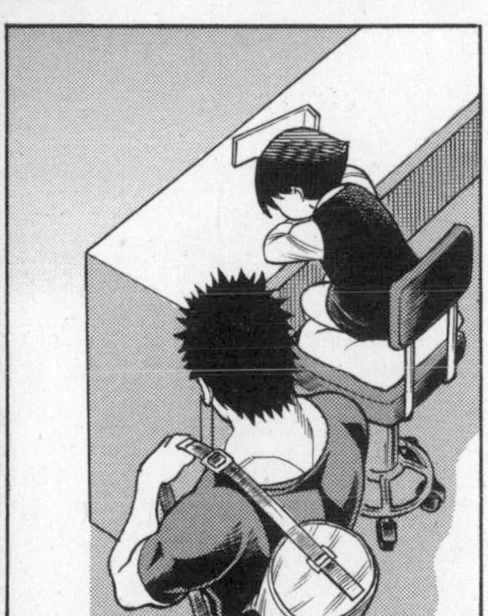

Acting Sheriff's Deputy

JIJI, COULD YOU LET ANNA KNOW I'M RELIEVING HER AS ACTING DEPUTY?
TELL HER THANKS FOR THE HELP.

AND TAKE THIS TO HIME-SAMA, OKAY?
GET IT TO HER AS FAST AS YOU CAN.

HAMA-OJI-CHAN ...
YOU'RE COMING HOME AGAIN, RIGHT?

WE'LL SEE YOU AGAIN SOON, *RIGHT* ?!

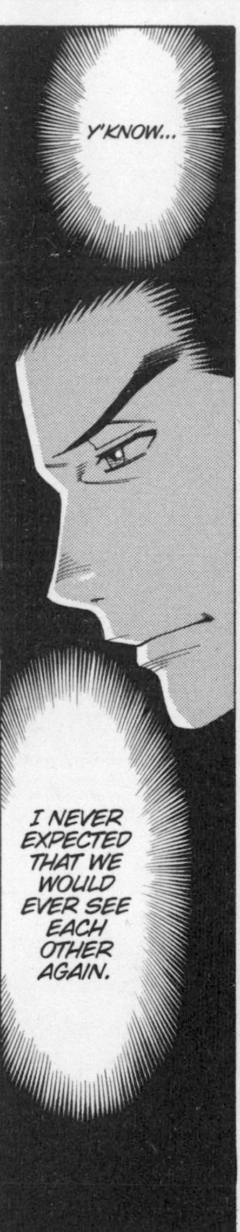
Y'KNOW...
I NEVER EXPECTED THAT WE WOULD EVER SEE EACH OTHER AGAIN.

I JUST KNEW GREAT THINGS WERE GOING TO HAPPEN TODAY.
MY HAIR BEHAVED, AND I COULD PUT IT IN EXACTLY THE WAVE I WANTED.
EVEN MY HOROSCOPE IN THE PAPER SAID TODAY WAS A LUCKY DAY FOR ME.

ALL OF IT WAS RIGHT.
I FINALLY FOUND THE ONE PERSON I'VE BEEN LOOKING FOR ALL THESE YEARS.

I'VE BECOME A DIPLOMAT.
I DECIDED TO DO THAT BECAUSE I THOUGHT IF I TRAVELLED AROUND THE WORLD, SOMEDAY I MIGHT STUMBLE ACROSS YOU. FUNNY, ISN'T IT? LAUGH IF YOU WANT.
UM... AM I TALKING TOO MUCH?
NO.

I NEVER THOUGHT I'D SEE YOU AGAIN.
HELL, I DIDN'T THINK YOU'D EVEN REMEMBER ME.
HA HA...
JUST KNOWING THAT YOU DID IS MORE THAN ENOUGH FOR ME.

......
I COULD NEVER FORGET!
YOU GAVE ME MY LIFE BACK.
I'LL REMEMBER YOU FOR THE REST OF MY LIFE.

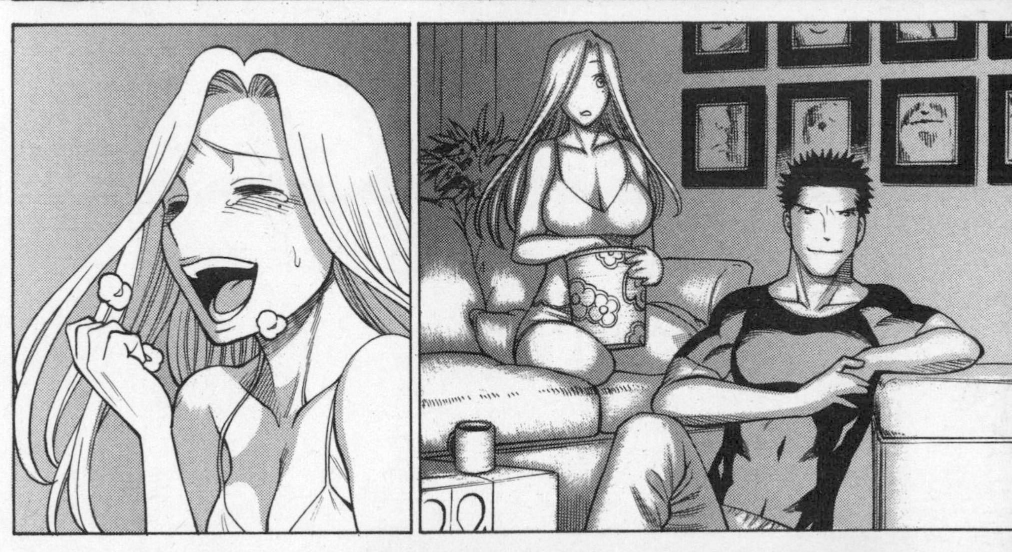

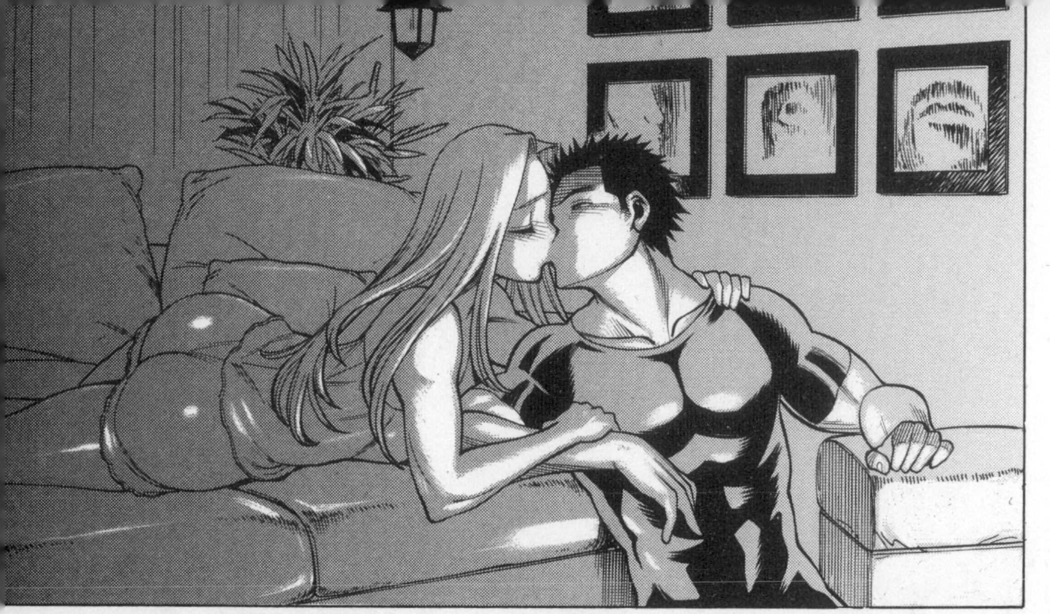

TODAY'S YOUR **BIRTHDAY,** RIGHT?
IS IT? I FORGOT.

OH, COME ON! HOW COULD YOU FORGET YOUR OWN BIRTHDAY?
WHAT KIND OF **PRESENT** DO YOU WANT?

A HAND-KER-CHIEF.

I LOST THE ONE FROM BEFORE.
A *HANKIE*? THAT'S ALL YOU WANT?
OKAY, THEN. I'LL GO PICK OUT THE PERFECT ONE FOR YOU!
!

SEE YOU TO-NIGHT!
I'LL PICK UP SOME WINE, TOO. SO BE GOOD AND WAIT FOR ME, OKAY?

GOODNESS, YOU *ARE* SUCH A TROUBLE-MAKER.
YOU COULD HARDLY CHOOSE A WORSE WOMAN TO ENTANGLE YOURSELF WITH. STILL... PERHAPS YOUR IGNORANCE OF WORLD AFFAIRS STEMS FROM YOUR LONG STAY OVERSEAS.

SO YOU'VE BEEN WATCHING ME?
YOU'RE FROM THE CLAN, THEN.

OF COURSE. IT WAS MY DUTY TO WATCH OVER YOU...
FWAP
AND TO PREVENT YOU FROM MAKING PRECISELY THIS SORT OF FOOLISH MISTAKE.

CNN REPORTER **NICOLE EDELMAN.**
THEY LOOK EXACTLY ALIKE, DON'T THEY? UNSURPRISING, AS SHE IS GOTOH REIKO'S TWIN SISTER. SHE IS PRESENTLY THE AUTHOR OF SEVERAL INVENTIVE PLOTS TO ACQUIRE SENSITIVE CLAN INFORMATION.
SHE'S REALLY RATHER FAMOUS. YOU CAN'T GO A DAY WITHOUT SEEING HER ON TV. ARE YOU SURE YOU NEVER KNEW?
DON'T GET TO WATCH MUCH TV OUT ON THE BATTLEFIELD.

HM. YOU DON'T SEEM TERRIBLY SHOCKED.

SO I GUESS VACATION'S OVER, EH?
NOT REALLY. I... JUST WANTED TO DREAM.
EVEN IF ONLY FOR A FEW DAYS.
CORRECT. THE CLAN HAS DISPATCHED NEW ORDERS FOR YOU.
THE LONG-RUMORED COLLABORATION BETWEEN THE ROYAL FAMILY AND THE JAPANESE GOVERNMENT HAS BECOME REALITY.
PROCEED TO JAPAN IMMEDIATELY AND JOIN WITH THE TRADITIONALISTS IN OPPOSITION TO THE TREATY. THERE, YOU ARE TO ASSEMBLE AND TRAIN AN ANTI-VAMPIRE TASK FORCE AS QUICKLY AS POSSIBLE.

RIIIING
RIIIING

RIIIING
NOKIA
REIKO
RIIIING

RIIIING
RIIIING
RIIIING

PLIP
NOKIA

I MEAN IT, HAMMER! WE'RE EVEN AFTER THIS!

SORRY, MAN. THIS IS THE LAST TIME.

AND TELL ME AHEAD OF TIME IF YOU'RE GONNA BE BRINGING GUYS ALONG!
I'LL START CHARGING YOU NEXT TIME!
?

OFF.
I CAN'T TAKE YOU WHERE I'M GOING.

WHAT, DON'T WANT BEOWULF OFFICIALLY ACCOMPANYING YOU ON PARAMILITARY ACTION?
RELAX. I HAVEN'T OFFICIALLY ACCEPTED MY COMMISSION, SO I'M NOT TECHNICALLY BEOWULF YET.

BAS-TARD.

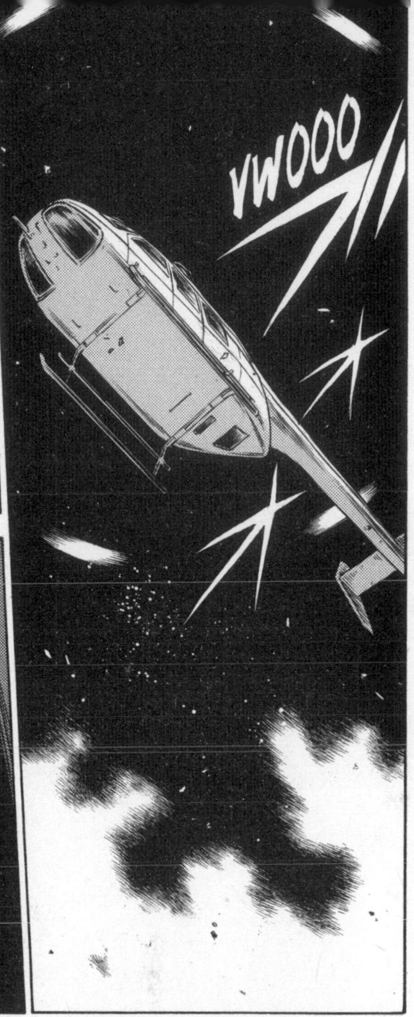
VWOOO

SET A COURSE GOING SOUTH. DUE SOUTH!
DUE SOUTH?! BUT THAT'LL TAKE US OUT OVER THE OCEAN!!

THE OCEAN?
WAIT... ARE YOU SAYING THEIR HIDEOUT IS ON THE SEA?

......

KREEAK
YOU DARED TO TALK BACK TO OUR HOLY MASTER IN A PITIFUL ATTEMPT TO BUY TIME? *HEH.*
FILTHY, SINFUL JEZEBEL.

IT LOOKS LIKE THE MASTER IS WILLING TO BE MERCIFUL AND GIVE YOU SOME TIME TO THINK ABOUT YOUR OPTIONS BEFORE QUESTIONING YOU.
YANK
OW ...!
BUT THAT'S MORE THAN A HERETIC HARLOT LIKE YOU DESERVES. WE'LL GET WHAT WE NEED QUICKER IF I JUST ASK THE **RIGHT KIND** OF QUESTIONS.

OUR ORGANIZATION HAS A WIDE VARIETY OF TOOLS THAT HAVE BEEN USED IN CENTURIES PAST.
SUCH AS *THIS.*
IT'S MEANT TO PUNISH LIARS. THIS END GOES INTO THEIR WRETCHED MOUTHS, AND YOU TURN THE SCREW HERE...
UNTIL IT OPENS SO FAR, THEIR JAWS SHATTER AND THEIR LIPS SPLIT OPEN TO THEIR NECK!
POK
BUT THERE ARE STILL A FEW SONGS WE NEED YOU TO SING, SO THIS MOUTH STAYS WHOLE. FOR NOW.
FORTU-NATELY, WOMEN HAVE TWO MOUTHS...
SWF
AND THIS LITTLE TOY HAPPENS TO BE *FAR MORE EFFECTIVE* WHEN USED ON THE LOWER ONE.
N-NO! DON'T!!
STOP!!

NOOOO!!
TAP TAP
SOK
WHUD

ELIE!
OWWW~!!

WAIT JUST A MINUTE, REIKO. I'LL GET THOSE OFF OF YOU.
YOU GOT OUT OF THOSE HAND-CUFFS...
HOW?

I CAN POP MY THUMB OUT OF JOINT PRETTY EASILY. SEE?
IT GOT THIS WAY THANKS TO HAMA'S MAGIC TRICKS.

IT'S BEEN, LIKE, FOREVER SINCE I LAST DID IT THOUGH, SO IT REALLY HURT!
HA HA ...

ALL RIGHT. WE NEED TO FIND A WAY OUT OF HERE.
IF WE CAN JUST BUY ENOUGH TIME...
HAMA-KUN WILL COME AND RESCUE US.
RIGHT!

Chapter 12: Bulletproof Soldier

GUARDS... AND THEY'VE GOT GUNS.

JEEZ, THERE ARE MORE OF THEM THAN I EXPECTED.
LET'S GO AROUND THE OTHER WAY.

UM, REIKO ?
YOU KNEW WHAT KIND OF **WORK** YOUR LATE FATHER DID, RIGHT?
ALL THAT RESEARCHING VAMPIRES AND STUFF.

I HAD AN IDEA, YES. THAT'S WHY HE GOT TOGETHER WITH MY MOTHER, AFTER ALL.
BUT I NEVER KNEW HE HAD PUT TOGETHER A **POWDER KEG** LIKE THE EDELMAN REPORT.

GRANDFATHER FORBADE EVEN TALKING ABOUT HIM, SO I DON'T KNOW ANYTHING ABOUT WHAT HE DID AFTER THE DIVORCE.
WELL, NOT THAT I KNOW MUCH ABOUT HIM FROM BEFORE THEN, EITHER.
ALL I REMEMBER IS THAT HE WAS GONE MOST OF THE TIME. WHEN HE CAME HOME, I'D ONLY SEE HIM ARGUING WITH MY MOTHER.

I CAN'T EVEN SAY IF HE REALLY DID MARRY MY MOTHER ONLY FOR THE SAKE OF HIS RESEARCH, AND IF HE FELT ANYTHING AT ALL FOR ME AND MY SISTER.
WELL, NO. HE *DID* TAKE NICOLE WITH HIM, SO I GUESS HE MUST HAVE FELT A LITTLE RESPONSIBILITY FOR US, AT LEAST.
BUT IF HE REALLY LOVED US...
DON'T YOU THINK HE WOULD HAVE DONE SOMETHING TO KEEP US OUT OF HIS MESSES, EVEN AFTER HE DIED?

REIKO ...

FWOOOO

TO

OH MY GOD!
WE'RE ON A SHIP!

REIKO, WHAT ARE WE GOING TO DO?!
I CAN'T SEE LAND!
NOT ANY-WHERE!
......

THE SUN IS JUST COMING UP.
WE WERE KIDNAPPED AFTER SEVEN O'CLOCK LAST NIGHT. THAT MEANS WE'VE PROBABLY BEEN ABOARD THIS SHIP FOR AROUND TEN HOURS. IF WE ASSUME WE'RE MOVING AT AN AVERAGE OF 20 KNOTS...
WE'RE PROBABLY AROUND THE EDGE OF THE EXCLUSIVE ECONOMIC ZONE, THEN.
HOW CAN YOU BE SO CALM?! WAY OUT ON THE OCEAN LIKE THIS, EVEN HAMA CAN'T COME AND SAVE US!!

AWWOOOOO
THEY'VE DISCOVERED WE'RE MISSING!
THIS WAY!
BUT WE'RE ON A BOAT! WHERE ARE WE GOING TO RUN TO?!
WE STILL HAVE TO BUY TIME! EVERY LITTLE BIT HELPS!!
BUY TIME? FOR WHAT?!
I ALREADY TOLD YOU!
HAMA-KUN WILL COME AND SAVE US, NO MATTER WHAT!!

A FREIGHT BARGE?!
BWOOOOO
THEIR HIDEOUT IS ON A SHIP?!

YEP. THE COLOMBIAN CONTAINER SHIP **CRUZ RODERIGO.**
IT PULLED OUT OF DOCK LAST NIGHT, HEADED STRAIGHT FOR GUAM!

GOD, THEY HAVE ACCESS TO SOMETHING LIKE THAT? THEIR ORGANIZATION HAS TO BE WAY BIGGER THAN WE THOUGHT.
BWOOOOOO
THEM? NO WAY. BUT THEIR BACKERS... YES.

WHEN THEY CUT THEMSELVES OFF FROM THE VATICAN, THEY WERE HOUNDED NEARLY TO EXTINCTION. BUT NOW, THEY'RE BACK AND CAPABLE OF OPERATING ON THIS LEVEL.
THEY'VE FOUND A NEW SPONSOR, AND A **BIG ONE** AT THAT!
IT'S PROBABLY THOSE BACKERS WHO ARE THE ONES REALLY AFTER THE EDELMAN REPORT.

TO TOP IT OFF, THAT CONTAINER SHIP IS OWNED BY AN AMERICAN THIRD-SECTOR COMPANY! THAT STINKS TO HIGH HEAVEN, DOESN'T IT?
GREAT...

*See Dance in the Vampire Bund Vol. 5, Chapter 31.

YOU HEARD THAT?
YEAH.
GOD. CAN'T EVER BE TOO CAREFUL AROUND YOU WERE-WOLVES.
WHEN MY MOM DIED, I THOUGHT IT WAS BECAUSE I HADN'T BEEN STRONG ENOUGH TO KEEP HER SAFE.
BUT MY UNCLE TOLD ME THAT REAL STRENGTH ISN'T MEASURED PHYSICALLY...
IT COMES FROM YOUR **SOUL.**

BUT BEFORE HE COULD TELL ME WHAT THAT REALLY MEANT, HE DIED TOO.
AGAIN, THERE WASN'T A DAMN THING I COULD DO TO SAVE HIM.
SO I ENLISTED IN THE ARMY.
I FIGURED THAT'D BE A PLACE THAT COULD TRAIN ME TO BE TRULY STRONG...

WENT FROM INFANTRY TO THE RANGERS, AND ALL THE WAY INTO **DELTA.**
BUT NO MATTER HOW HIGH I CLIMBED UP IN THE RANKS, I STILL HAD SO MANY THINGS I COULD LOSE.
MY MEN. MY FRIENDS.
MY PARTNER, WHO FOLLOWED ME THROUGH HELL AND BACK A DOZEN TIMES.
MY SENSE OF SELF...

EVEN...
EVEN NICOLE...

—TWO YEARS PRIOR, THE EVE OF THE BUND'S OFFICIAL OPENING, A TOKYO RESTAURANT.—
WE PROVIDED YOU WITH PLENTY OF MEN AND PLENTY OF TIME IN WHICH TO TRAIN THEM.
DESPITE ALL THAT, ARE YOU ATTEMPTING TO TELL US THAT YOUR UNIT IS NOT FULLY PREPARED FOR ACTION?

THE OFFICIAL ANNOUNCEMENT HAS NOT YET BEEN MADE, BUT THE NEW SPECIAL DISTRICT IS ALREADY FULLY FUNCTIONAL!
IT WILL NOT BE LONG BEFORE PRINCESS MINA ATTEMPTS TO MOVE HER ENTIRE RETINUE INTO IT.
OUR WAR HAS BEGUN!

DO YOU EVEN COMPRE-HEND THAT?
WE WILL NOT BE TOLD THAT OUR ANTI-VAMPIRE STRIKE FORCE ISN'T READY!
I DO UNDER-STAND, SIR.
AND I ASSURE YOU, THE MEN HAVE BEEN TRAINED TO THE GREATEST EXTENT POSSIBLE WITHIN THE TIME FRAME PROVIDED. THEIR MORALE IS ALSO VERY HIGH.
WHAT WE LACK IS APPROPRIATE EQUIPMENT.

ARE YOU SAYING THE EQUIPMENT WE PROVIDED IS *INSUFFICIENT?*
IT WOULD BE MORE THAN SUFFICIENT, SIR, IF WE WERE FACING A HUMAN FORCE.
HOWEVER, OUR OPPONENTS ARE *VAMPIRES.*
AND IF THIS UNIT'S TRUE MISSION IS THE ASSASSINATION OF MINA-HIME HERSELF...
IF YOU DO NOT UPGRADE OUR EQUIPMENT, SIR, WE WILL BE **CRUSHED.**

YES, BUT ...
FROM ARMORED VEHICLES TO ATTACK HELICOPTERS, THIS LIST IS **LUDICROUS.**
ANTI-TANK RIFLES? ROCKET LAUNCHERS?
WHERE DO YOU EXPECT US TO FIND THAT SORT OF HEAVY ARMAMENT INSIDE JAPAN?
YES, YES.
BUT APACHE ATTACK HELICOPTERS? STRYKER ARMORED FIGHTING VEHICLES?
THESE THINGS HARDLY GROW ON TREES.
THE VAMPIRE ROYAL FAMILY IS GUARDED BY A FULLY-ARMED, ELITE MILITARY UNIT, SIR. TO BE PERFECTLY FRANK, THAT LIST IS STILL SHORT SEVERAL NECESSARY THINGS.
I HAVE ALREADY SENT INQUIRIES TO CLAN ROZENMANN'S OFFICES IN THE UNITED STATES. AS LONG AS WE CAN SECURE YOUR **APPROVAL,** THEY WILL IMMEDIATELY BEGIN ACQUIRING THEM.

DON'T GET THE WRONG IDEA.
WE WERE ALREADY IN AN EXCELLENT POSITION TO ASSEMBLE OUR OWN ANTI-VAMPIRE UNIT, *WITHOUT* ANY AID FROM YOU OR YOUR CLAN.

HOWEVER, ON THE REQUEST OF THE AMERICAN GOVERNMENT, OUR PARTY LEADERSHIP INFORMED US WE ARE TO GIVE DEFERENCE TO YOUR CLAN. THAT IS THE *ONLY REASON* WHY WE HAVE ACCEPTED YOUR ASSIGNMENT.
WE HAVE GIVEN YOU AS MANY CONCES-SIONS AS YOU WILL GET.

YET NOW, YOU ASK US TO ACQUIRE *RIDICULOUSLY EXPENSIVE* ARMY TOYS--TOYS WHICH ARE *FROWNED UPON* BY OUR NATIONAL LAWS, I MIGHT ADD--AND BUY THEM FROM YOUR OWN CLAN? *HA!*
THERE MAY BE MANY WEALTHY PEOPLE IN THE FINANCIAL WORLD WHO AGREE WITH OUR POSITION, BUT THEY ARE NOT BOTTOMLESS WELLS OF MONEY!
......

SHEESH. THESE JAPANESE POLITICAL TYPES HAVE DOZENS OF FANCY OFFICES AND MEETING ROOMS ALL OVER THE PLACE, BUT SOMEHOW THEY ALWAYS WANNA DO BUSINESS AT A RESTAURANT.
WHY IS THAT?
WHO KNOWS...
MAYBE THEY JUST AREN'T SATISFIED UNLESS THEY'RE SHOVING SOMETHING INTO THEIR MOUTHS. THEY'RE A GREEDY ENOUGH BUNCH FOR ME TO BELIEVE IT.

RIIING

!

SORRY, SOMETHING JUST CAME UP. DROP ME OFF. ANY-WHERE'S OKAY.
I'LL TAKE YOU SOME-WHERE CLOSE. IS SOME-THING UP?

NAH. AN OLD FRIEND CALLED TO VISIT...

THAT MAN IS BECOMING A BIGGER AND BIGGER ANNOY-ANCE.
SIR ...

WE HAVE HEARD ...
THAT AT A LATER HOUR TONIGHT, ON THE OUTSKIRTS OF TAMA, ALL THE POLITICAL AND FINANCIAL BACKERS OF THE TEPES FACTION WILL BE GATHERING FOR A SOCIAL.

BAM
DAMN THAT OLD MAN ISURUGI!
HE'S ACTING LIKE THE WHOLE WORLD IS HIS OYSTER!

THEY'RE ALL COMING TOGETHER? WHAT A PERFECT OPPORTUNITY.
THAT MAN DID SAY WHAT WE HAVE RIGHT NOW IS PLENTY FOR *HUMAN* OPPONENTS.

HRM. RIGHT NOW, WE CANNOT SAY FOR CERTAIN HOW FAR THE TEPES FACTION HAS INFILTRATED OUR GOVERNMENT.

IF THEY ARE ALL GOING TO BE IN ONE PLACE, IT GIVES US AN EXCELLENT CHANCE TO CLEAN HOUSE ENTIRELY...

YOU THERE!
IS IT POSSIBLE TO MOBILIZE THE UNIT WITHOUT GETTING THAT MAN'S PERMISSION?!
IT IS DIFFICULT, BUT *POSSIBLE*, SIR...
EXCELLENT! DO IT!!

WANT ME TO WAIT?
NAH, YOU GO ON HOME. I'LL BE BACK LATER TONIGHT.

RIIING
HN?
NOW IT'S *MY* PHONE RINGING...

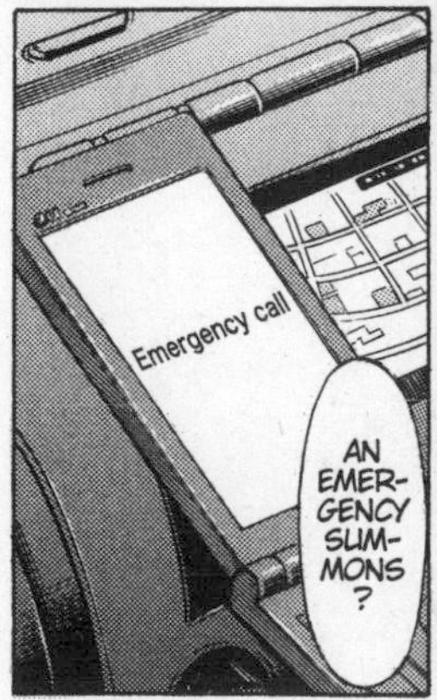
Emergency call
AN EMERGENCY SUMMONS?

HEY, HAM- MER!
DAMN... HE'S ALREADY GONE.
SEIJI...
TAP TAP

YOU NOTICED.
SO THAT'S WHY YOU LEFT NEW YORK SO SUDDENLY.

WHEN DID YOU ARRIVE IN JAPAN?
JUST RECENTLY. I CAME HERE AS QUICKLY AS I COULD. THERE'S SOMETHING I HAVE TO TELL YOU...

THE REASON WHY YOU PRE-TENDED TO BE YOUR SISTER?
OR ARE YOU HERE TO SQUEEZE WHATEVER INFO YOU CAN GET OUT OF ME ON CLAN ROZEN-MANN?

NO!
I'D NEVER DO THAT!

I...
I JUST WANTED TO MEET YOU FOR MYSELF.

I WANTED TO SEE THE MAN WHO SAVED MY SISTER WITH MY OWN EYES.

WE WERE SEPARATED WHEN WE WERE ONLY TEN YEARS OLD. I HAVEN'T BEEN ALLOWED TO SEE HER SINCE THEN.
BUT WE'VE KEPT IN TOUCH SECRETLY, THROUGH EMAIL...
THIS WHOLE TIME.

SO I KNOW ABOUT THE SOLDIER WHO RISKED HIS LIFE TO SAVE HER IN AFGHANISTAN.
JO-- SHE BARELY SAW HIS FACE PAST THE HELMET AND THE GOGGLES, AND HE NEVER SPOKE MUCH, BUT SHE STILL FELL FOR HIM. SHE'D GIVE *ANYTHING* TO SEE HIM AGAIN.
SHE'S TOLD ME THE STORY SO MANY TIMES, IT'S BECOME A PART OF ME NOW, TOO.

SO WHEN I WAS READING ROZENMANN'S FILES ON THEIR ARTIFICIAL BEAST-MAN PROJECT AND THE HISTORY OF THE EX-SOLDIER WHO WAS THEIR LONE SUCCESS, MY HEART ALMOST STOPPED.
HE WAS DISHONOR-ABLY DIS-CHARGED AFTER GOING AGAINST ORDERS TO RESCUE A GIRL IN AFGHANI-STAN.
I KNEW HE HAD TO BE THE ONE.
SO YOU WENT TO SEE ME IN NEW YORK...
DELIBER-ATELY PLAYING IT OFF AS A CHANCE ENCOUN-TER.
I HAD PLANNED TO TELL YOU THAT I WAS HER SISTER.
I NEVER EXPECTED THERE'D BE ANYONE WHO WOULDN'T KNOW BY SIGHT CNN'S MOST FAMOUS REPORTER.

BUT YOU DIDN'T NOTICE.
I... I COULDN'T HELP MYSELF.

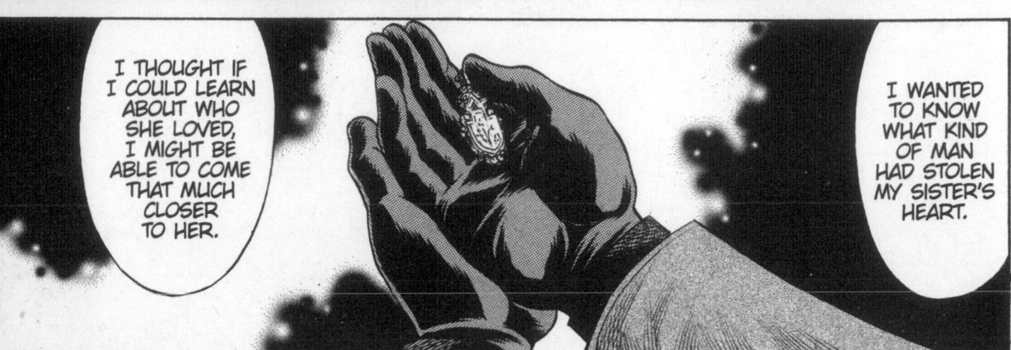
I WANTED TO KNOW WHAT KIND OF MAN HAD STOLEN MY SISTER'S HEART.
I THOUGHT IF I COULD LEARN ABOUT WHO SHE LOVED, I MIGHT BE ABLE TO COME THAT MUCH CLOSER TO HER.

AND DID YOU?
YES. I KNOW ALL TOO WELL NOW.
SHF
I'D GIVE UP EVERY-THING IN A HEART-BEAT...
IF ONLY YOU'D COME WITH ME.

I CAN'T DO THAT.
WHY?! IS YOUR MISSION FOR ROZEN-MANN THAT IMPORTANT?!
NO, NICOLE.
YOU KNOW WHY.
JO...
I NEVER THOUGHT I WOULD BE THIS JEALOUS OF HER.
SQUEEZE
BUT FOR NOW...
JUST FOR RIGHT NOW... STAY WITH ME.

SOMETHING ISN'T RIGHT HERE, NICOLE. YOU'RE ACTING FUNNY!
WHAT IS IT?! WHY DID YOU REALLY COME TO JAPAN?!
NICOLE?!

THE ORGANIZATION I BELONG TO LEAKED SOME INFORMATION TO YOUR EMPLOYERS.
BUT THAT INFORMATION IS FAKE.
THEY PLAN TO USE YOUR ASSASSINATION ATTEMPT AS A DIVERSION.
THE ONLY THING WAITING FOR YOU THERE IS DEATH.
THEY ARE PROBABLY MOBILIZING YOUR UNIT AS WE SPEAK.
I... I WANTED TO SAVE YOU.
I DON'T WANT YOU TO DIE. I COULDN'T BEAR IT...
THAT'S WHY I CAME...

WHIRL
SEIJI?!
SEIJI!!
THAT DAY...
IF ONLY I HADN'T LET GO OF HER HAND, THEN MAYBE...

THIS TIME...
I WON'T LET GO.

HAVE YOU STILL NOT FOUND THEM?
N-NO, SIR! TH-THEY MUST HAVE FOUND SOME NOOK SOME-WHERE...

WHAT A FUTILE EFFORT.
WE ARE ON THE OCEAN. WHERE DO THEY THINK THEY CAN RUN?

AH, WELL. TELL THE MERCENARIES TO CHASE THEM DOWN, BUT NOT TO KILL THEM.
AS LONG AS THEY REMAIN ALIVE, THE SOLDIERS CAN HAVE A LITTLE FUN WITH THEM.

THAT MAY LOOSEN HER TIGHT LIPS.
SPANG
SPA-SPANG
KYAAA!
SPOK
SPOK
BRAT-TAT-TAT
N-NO!
KYAAAA!
ELIE, YOU HAVE TO MOVE!
AAAAH!!
THIS WAY, ELIE!!
AAAH!
WE HAVE TO RUN AWAY!

W-WE'RE GONNA DIE!
THERE WAS A "POP-POP-POP" SOUND AND A REALLY BRIGHT FLASH, A-AND HAMA STARTED BLEEDING ...!
H-HE WAS BLEEDING! THEY GOT HIM, REIKO! THEY SHOT HAMA!
AAAAAAAH!!
BLAM BLAM BLAM
NGH...!
JUST LIKE THE DRIVER, MIGUEL, DID!
A-AND THE BISHOP ...!
ELIE!
SHE MUST BE RELIVING HER CHILDHOOD TRAUMA ...!
SPAK SPAK SPAK
'EY, WE'RE ALLOWED TO DO WHATEVER WE WANT, AS LONG AS WE DON'T KILL 'EM, RIGHT?
DIP-SHIT...
QUIT IT WITH THAT RIFLE SHIT ALREADY. WE CAN'T AFFORD TO GRAZE THESE BITCHES.
I KNOW, MAN! I KNOW! BUT GODDAMN, YOU REMEMBER BACK IN KINSHASA? THAT WAS SOME HOT PUSSY, MAN.
AFTER THE WHOLE GROUP OF US HAD OUR FUN WITH 'EM, WE WENT AROUND AND SHOT EACH OF 'EM ONCE IN THE RIGHT ARM, THEN THE LEFT ARM...

HOW MANY SHOTS DID IT TAKE FOR THAT ONE CHICK?
HOW MANY *HOURS* WAS IT AGAIN?
HEH. DON'T REMEMBER.
OKAY, THEN. WE'LL START WITH YOU.
LET'S HAVE SOME FUN.
WSH
BAAANG
YWOOOOM
SPLUK

CHOOM
CHOOM
CHOOM
CHOOM
CHOOM
HAMA-KUN!!!

I'M GOING DOWN THERE!
BACK ME UP!
CHIMM
CHIMM
ROGER!
WOOOSH
WHAK

KEEP FLYING AROUND THE PERI-METER LIKE THIS!
CHMM CHMM CHMM
ROGER, DAMMIT! HAMMER ALWAYS DRAGS ME INTO THIS SHIT!!
BLAM
BLAM
BRAT-TAT TAT
BLAM
BLAM
WE'RE RAPIDLY NEARING THE POINT OF NO RETURN! IF YOU WANNA GET BACK ALIVE, FINISH THIS UP FAST!
ROGER!
GOTOH-SAN!!
SPANG
SPANG
CHMM CHMM CHMM

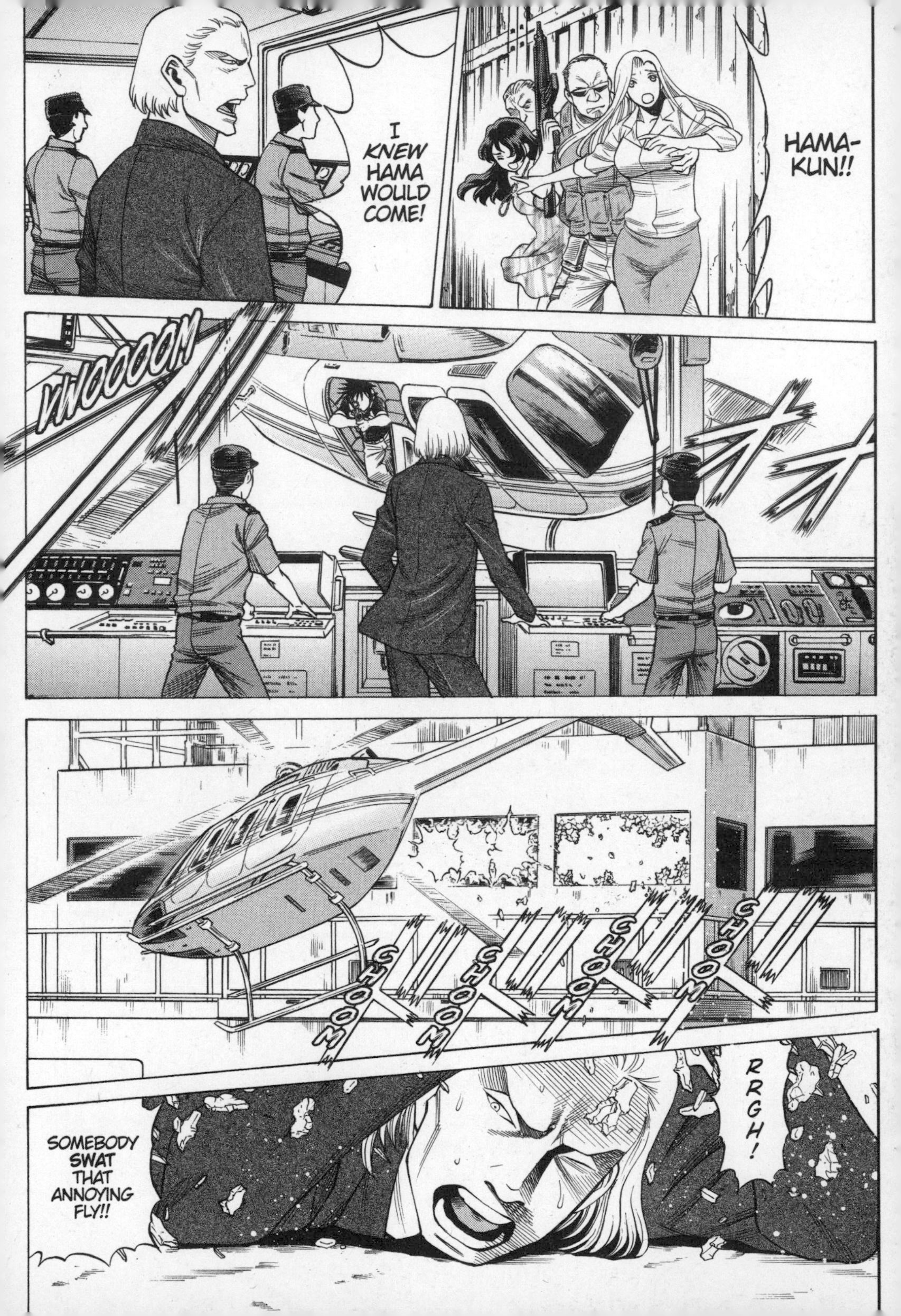
HAMA-KUN!!
I KNEW HAMA WOULD COME!
VWOOOOM
CHOOM
CHOOM
CHOOM
CHOOM
RRGH!
SOMEBODY SWAT THAT ANNOYING FLY!!

KREE
KREE
KCHUNK
GRUMMM
WHRANG
CHUT
CHUT
WHRANG
WHRANG
CHUT
CHUT
BWOOF
WHRR
WHRR
WHRR
AKIRA!!
GAAAAH!!
KRISH
KRASH

HAMMER!!

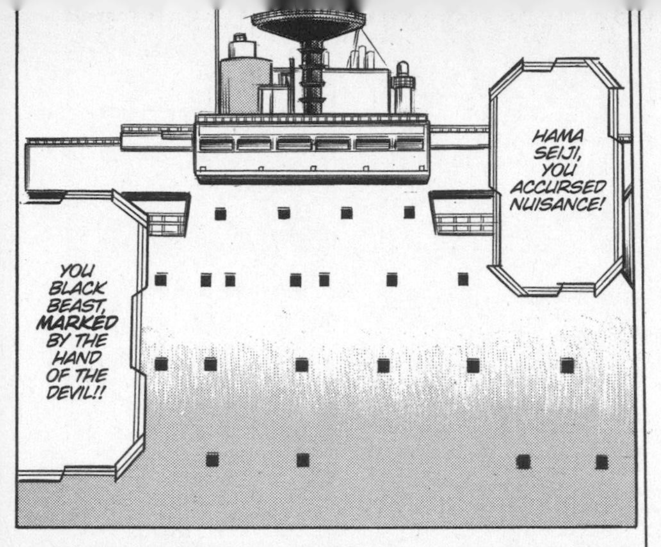
HAMA SEIJI, YOU ACCURSED NUISANCE!
YOU BLACK BEAST, **MARKED** BY THE HAND OF THE DEVIL!!

I THOUGHT YOU MIGHT COME THIS FAR!
I KNEW YOUR SINGLE-MINDED DESIRE TO SAVE THE EDELMAN HARLOT WOULD **DRIVE YOU** TO IT!!

SO I TOOK THE LIBERTY OF PREPARING AN APPROPRIATE **WELCOME** FOR YOU!
CHOK
CHOK
DOZENS OF NOTORIOUS MERCENARIES ARE STANDING IN YOUR WAY!

IF YOU WANT THE WOMAN BACK, YOU WILL HAVE TO FIGHT AND CLAW YOUR WAY THROUGH THEIR RANKS!
THIS IS ASSUMING SHE IS STILL ALIVE BY THE TIME YOU REACH HER!
!
SKRRR..
BOLTON ...
BOLTON, CAN YOU HEAR ME?
MASTER BOLTON! OVER THERE!

TAKE A GOOD LOOK AT ME, BOLTON.
AH! THAT'S --!
GIVE ME THAT!
!!
THERE WERE TWO PENDANTS.
ONE FOR THE OLDER SISTER, AND ONE FOR THE YOUNGER.

LOOKS LIKE YOU PULLED THE WRONG TICKET.
I'VE GOT THE WINNER RIGHT HERE.
WHA?
RRGH ...!
GRAAAAAH!!
WHAT...? **HAMA-KUN** HAS NICOLE'S PENDANT?
BUT WHY?!

THINGS SURE HAVE GOTTEN INTERESTING, EH?
YOU'VE GOT ELIE AND GOTOH-SAN. I'VE GOT THE PENDANT. WE'RE EACH HOLDING JUST WHAT THE OTHER WANTS MOST.

THAT MEANS THERE'S ONLY ONE THING FOR US TO DO.
NO CLEVER PLANS, NO FUNNY BUSINESS. JUST YOU AND ME, WINNER TAKES ALL. WELL?
HE IS *INSANE* ...

AS YOU WISH.
THERE ARE ENOUGH MERCENARIES ON THIS SHIP TO FORM A FULL COMPANY.
BUT ARE YOU SURE YOU WANT TO TAKE ON THIS BATTLE AS **HANDICAPPED** AS YOU ARE?
HANDI-CAPPED?

DO YOU REALLY THINK YOU CAN BEAT THEM ALL?
ESPE-CIALLY...

IN YOUR CURRENT... **UNSTABLE CONDITION?**
!

THAT CORRUPT FLESH OF YOURS, BUILT AND REBUILT, IS REACHING ITS LIMITS.
IN FACT, IT HAS GOTTEN SO BAD THAT WITHOUT REGULAR DOSES OF A CERTAIN DRUG, IT CAN NO LONGER SUPPORT YOUR LIFE.
HEH HEH... HOW DO I KNOW THAT?
I KNOW EVERYTHING ABOUT YOU!
OUR ORGANIZATION HAS ENSURED THAT EVERY ONE OF ROZENMANN'S FACILITIES IN THE UNITED STATES HAS BEEN CRUSHED.
WHEN WAS THE LAST TIME YOU TOOK YOUR "MEDICINE," HAMA?
IT HAS TO HAVE BEEN SOME TIME NOW. WELL? WHEN YOUR NEXT SEIZURE STRIKES...
NO ...!
I EXPECT IT WILL BE YOUR LAST, AND YOUR SOUL WILL GUTTER AND GO OUT LIKE A SPENT CANDLE.

WHO KNOWS?
WE WON'T KNOW THE WINNER 'TIL WE ROLL THE DICE.

HA! EVEN NOW, YOU CAN'T RESIST GETTING THE LAST WORD.
ALL RIGHT.

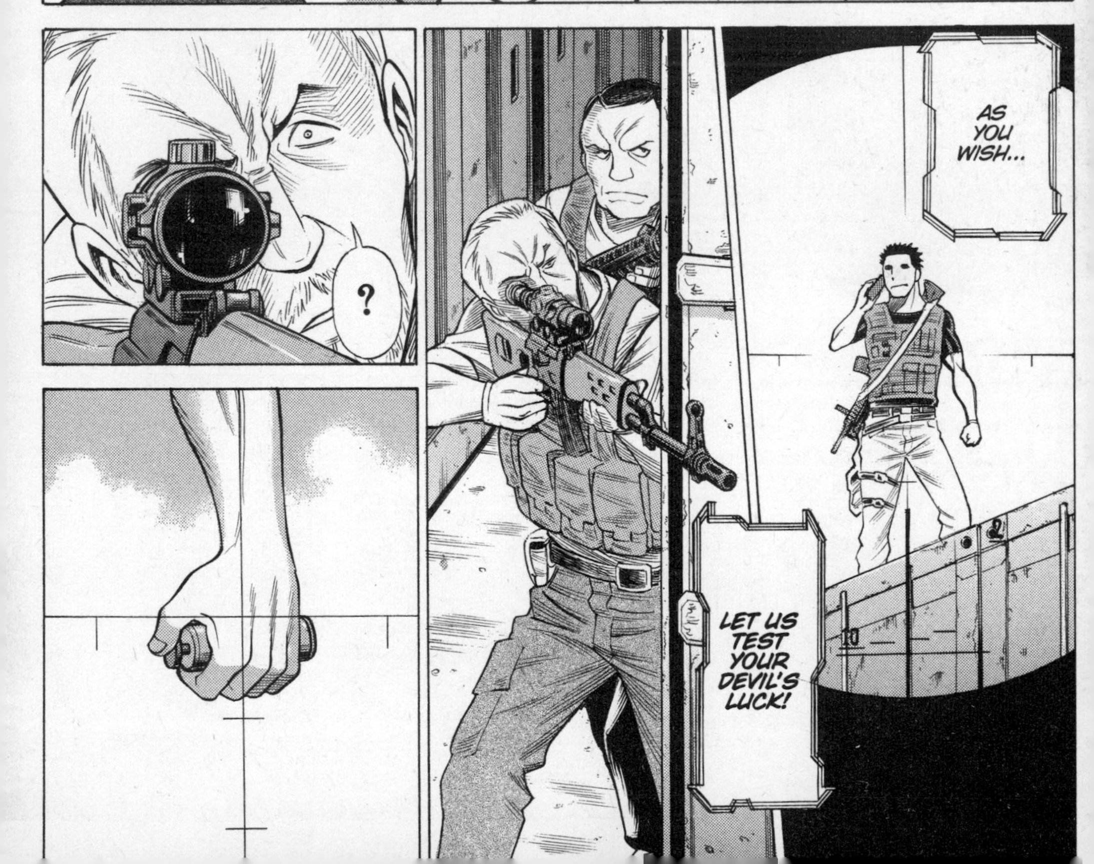
AS YOU WISH...
?
LET US TEST YOUR DEVIL'S LUCK!

KLIK
カチ
BEEEEEEE
FOOM
BOOM
BOOM
BOOM

RUMBL
RUMBL
RUMBL

KLONG
KLONG
KLONG
Chapter 13: Someday, This Love...
KLNG
KLNG
KLNG
KLNG
SPBLOOOOOOSH
SIR, WE'RE LISTING STARBOARD! AT THIS RATE, WE ARE GOING TO CAPSIZE!
STEER PORTSIDE IMMEDI-ATELY! HARD PORT!!
HAMAAA!!

BRAT-TAT-TAT-TAT-TAT
TMP
SKSHHHH
WHUNCH

THOOOOOM
NO, NOT YET ...!
IT'S WAY TOO SOON!

BLAM

HEY, HAMA-SAN!
AKIRA! YOU'RE OKAY!
HELL, YEAH! THAT WAS NOTHING!
"NOTHING," MY ASS! I NEARLY GOT *KILLED*!!

HAMA-SAN, YOU CAN'T TAKE MUCH MORE OF THIS. NOT IN YOUR CONDITION.
YOU HANG BACK. WE'LL GET GOTOH-SAN.

CLUTCH
CAN'T DO THAT...
IT'S GOTTA BE **ME.**
YOU KNOW THAT.
HAMA-SAN...

BESIDES...
*I'VE GOT A **FAVOR** I WANNA ASK YOU.*
!

SIR. WE HAVE SUCCESSFULLY HALTED THE LIST FOR NOW, WITH A RECALIBRATION OF OUR BALLAST.
GRUMMMMM
*HOWEVER, SHOULD WE EXPERIENCE ANY FURTHER TILT, IT COULD LEAVE US DEAD IN THE WATER. IN A WORST CASE SCENARIO, WE MIGHT EVEN **CAPSIZE.***
GRUMMMMM

WHERE ARE WE NOW?
WE ARE A FEW KILOMETERS SHORT OF THE EDGE OF JAPAN'S EEZ.

DO NOT LET THIS SHIP SINK. UNDER-STOOD?
GOOD.

HE CAME...
HE REALLY CAME.

YOU WERE RIGHT, REIKO!
HAMA REALLY CAME TO SAVE US!

SEE? I KNEW THIS WOULD HAPPEN.

EVER SINCE THAT DAY, MORE THAN TEN YEARS AGO...
HE'S BEEN MY GUARDIAN ANGEL.
REIKO ...

HMPH. SO THAT DEVIL-BEAST THINKS HE'S AN ANGEL, NOW?
THAT ALONE IS ENOUGH TO CONDEMN HIM TO A THOUSAND PAINFUL DEATHS.
WHAT A FOOL. GOING THIS FAR, ALL FOR THE SAKE OF A MERE WOMAN.
BUT THAT IS PERFECT FOR ME.
THAT FOOLISHNESS FINALLY GIVES ME THE CHANCE TO EXACT THE REVENGE I HAVE BEEN WAITING *YEARS* FOR!

THE REVENGE THAT I HAVE DESERVED...
SINCE THAT DAY IN THE AFGHAN DESERTS!
YES. I DO SPEAK OF TEN YEARS AGO...
WHEN YOU WERE ABDUCTED AND SHOULD HAVE BEEN EXECUTED.
I BET YOU STILL BELIEVE IT, DON'T YOU?
YOU THINK THAT WAS SIMPLY ANOTHER COMMON EXAMPLE OF AFGHAN GUERILLAS ABDUCING FOREIGN NATIONALS FOR THEIR OWN TERRORIST AGENDAS.
BUT IT WASN'T!
IT ALL STARTED WITH YOUR FATHER, JONAS EDELMAN.
THAT HATEFUL, CONNIVING HACK OF A JOURNALIST!

DID YOU TRULY THINK THAT ONE MAN COULD INVESTIGATE ALL THE MYRIAD BRANCHES OF THE VAMPIRES' CONNECTIONS WITH HUMAN SOCIETY?!
NO! THAT WAS ONLY POSSIBLE BECAUSE HE HAD THE SPONSORSHIP AND BACKING OF OUR ORGANIZATION!
HE CREATED THE EDELMAN REPORT BY **OUR ORDER!**

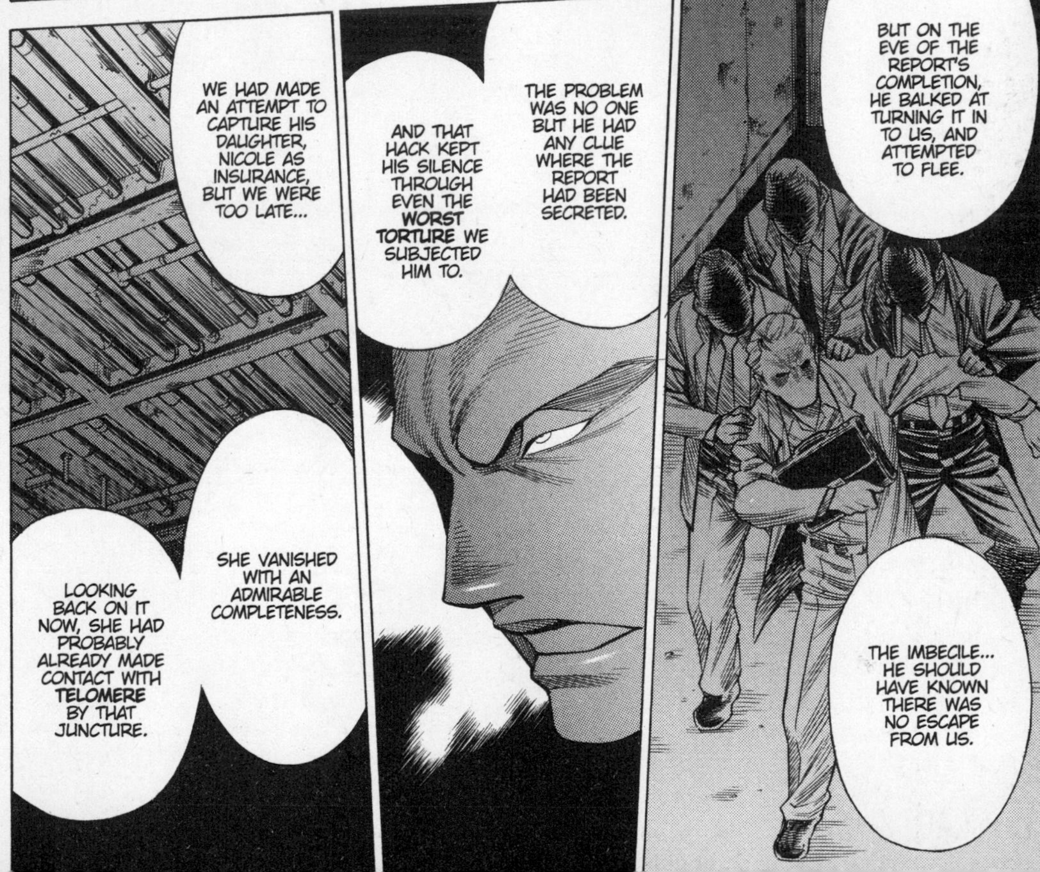
BUT ON THE EVE OF THE REPORT'S COMPLETION, HE BALKED AT TURNING IT IN TO US, AND ATTEMPTED TO FLEE.
THE IMBECILE... HE SHOULD HAVE KNOWN THERE WAS NO ESCAPE FROM US.
THE PROBLEM WAS NO ONE BUT HE HAD ANY CLUE WHERE THE REPORT HAD BEEN SECRETED.
AND THAT HACK KEPT HIS SILENCE THROUGH EVEN THE **WORST TORTURE** WE SUBJECTED HIM TO.
WE HAD MADE AN ATTEMPT TO CAPTURE HIS DAUGHTER, NICOLE AS INSURANCE, BUT WE WERE TOO LATE...
SHE VANISHED WITH AN ADMIRABLE COMPLETENESS.
LOOKING BACK ON IT NOW, SHE HAD PROBABLY ALREADY MADE CONTACT WITH **TELOMERE** BY THAT JUNCTURE.

THAT LEFT *YOU* AS OUR ONE REMAINING OPTION.
WE WERE AWARE THE CHANCES THAT YOU KNEW ANYTHING OF RELEVANCE WERE SLIM TO NONE. HOWEVER, YOU COULD BE VERY USEFUL AS A TOOL TO MAKE JONAS BREAK HIS SILENCE.

REIKO!

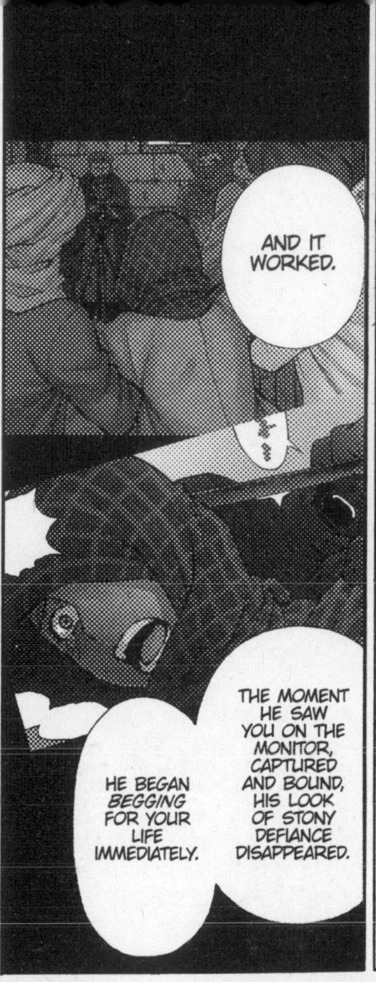
AND IT WORKED.
THE MOMENT HE SAW YOU ON THE MONITOR, CAPTURED AND BOUND, HIS LOOK OF STONY DEFIANCE DISAPPEARED.
HE BEGAN *BEGGING* FOR YOUR LIFE IMMEDIATELY.

YOU WERE NOT ABDUCTED BY GUERILLAS, HARLOT.
THEY WERE ALL MERCE-NARIES I HIRED PERSON-ALLY.

FATHER DID WHAT ...?!
TO BE HONEST, HE WAS *THIS CLOSE* TO TELLING ME WHERE THE REPORT WAS HIDDEN.

THIS! CLOSE!
BUT THEN HE BARGED IN AND RUINED EVERYTHING!
WHEN JONAS SAW HIM SHOOTING DOWN MY MEN...
BLAM
HE CLOSED HIS MOUTH FOR GOOD!!
NO MATTER HOW EXCRUCIATING THE TORTURE, HE NEVER SAID ANOTHER WORD!
NOT EVEN WHEN HE FINALLY DIED DID THAT SMUG SMILE OF TRIUMPH LEAVE HIS FACE!!

DURING THE TEN YEARS SINCE THEN, THE EDELMAN REPORT HAS REMAINED MISSING!
ALL BE-CAUSE OF HIM!
EVERY-THING WOULD HAVE WORKED, IF ONLY HE HADN'T COME!!

KCHAK-CHAK
MAN, YOU MAKE IT SOUND LIKE YOU WERE THERE.
HEH. I WAS.
I WAS THERE...
IN THAT RAM-SHACKLE HUT.
I WAS THERE!
WHEN YOU BARGED IN, GUN BLAZING...
AND STOLE HER OUT OF MY HANDS !!

HIM?!
THAT WAS YOU?!
BLAM
BLAM
BLAM

CHASE HIM DOWN!
SURROUND HIM AND WEAR HIM DOWN!
BUT TAKE YOUR TIME! THERE IS NO NEED TO RUSH!
THAT BEAST IS ON THE LAST OF HIS NINE LIVES!!
HFF ...!
HFF ...!
HAMA-KUN!!

WATCH CLOSELY, HARLOT!
TAT- TAT
TAT- TAT-
WATCH THE PITIFUL END OF THE MAN WHOSE LIFE YOU DESTROYED!!
WOE UNTO YOU!
YOU, WHO INVITED ADAM TO TASTE OF THE FORBIDDEN FRUIT!
YOU, WHO TOOK HIS HAND AND LED HIM ON THE PATH OF EXILE FROM PARADISE!!
DECEPTION, THY NAME IS WOMAN!!
GOD, WHAT'S WITH ALL THE THEATRICS ...?
AND YOU LIFTED THAT LAST LINE ALMOST COMPLETELY FROM SHAKESPEARE.

BOLTON, HOW ABOUT I SET YOU STRAIGHT ON ONE THING?
YEAH, I'M ON MY LAST LEGS, BUT NOT IN THE WAY YOU THINK.
GRIK
GRIK
IT'S NOT MY LIFE I'M ON THE VERGE OF LOSING... IT'S MY ABILITY TO HOLD HUMAN SHAPE!
BOOOOM
GRIK
GRIK

GOTOH-SAN... I REALLY WISH I DIDN'T HAVE TO SHOW YOU THIS...!
FIRE!
FIRE!!
BLAM
BLAM
BLAM
HAMA-KUN!!!

UNCLE ...
WHOOSH
EVEN UP TO THE VERY END, I NEVER GOT WHAT YOU SAID...
GRIK
AT ALL !!
GRAWR

KRUNCH

BRUP-UP-UP
BRAT-TAT-TAT-TAT
WSH

GET THAT TANK OUT HERE!
NOW!!
THMM
ST-STAY BACK!
KRUNCH
SPLAT
SPLAT
KRAK
KRUK
I'LL DO IT!! I'LL--
THMM

ELIE!
GOTOH-SAN!
THIS WAY!
WHUNK
GROOOAAARRR

NO WAY... NO WAY!!
THAT CAN'T BE HAMA... IT JUST CAN'T!!
C'MON, WE NEED TO GET GOING. HAMA-SAN ASKED ME TO TAKE CARE OF YOU TWO.
I'LL GET YOU OFF THIS SHIP.
BUT WHAT ABOUT HAMA-KUN?! HOW IS HE GETTING OFF?!

HE... HE *WON'T*. HE SAID HE WANTS TO GO DOWN WITH THE SHIP.
!

WHAT?! WE HAVE TO STOP HIM!!
WE CAN'T. NOT ANYMORE.
BESIDES...

THE LEAST YOU CAN DO FOR HIM IS THE FAVOR OF NOT SEEING HIM LIKE THAT.
PLEASE.

THMM
THMM
CHOOOM
CHOOOM
CHOOOM
CHOOM
CHOOM
GRUM
GRUM
CHOOM
CHOOM

SPOK
SPOK
SPOK
AFTER HIM!!
DO NOT SLOW DOWN!!
GRUM
GRUM
SPOK
SPOK
SPOK
GRMMMMM
THIS IS THE BRIDGE! WHAT THE HELL IS GOING ON DOWN THERE?!
TMP
THE SHIP CAN'T TAKE ANY MORE OF THIS!! CEASE FIRE! CEASE FIRE!!

WOOSH
GRUM
GRUM
GRUM
TMP
SHUT UP!!
CHOOM
CHOOM
CHOOM
CHOOM
OR I MAY NEVER HAVE THE CHANCE AGAIN!
I HAVE TO FINISH OFF THAT FLEA-BITTEN BEAST NOW...

DON'T RELY ON THE CAN-NONS!
RAM HIM HARD AND PIN HIM!!
CHOOM
CHOOM
CHOOM
CHOOM
CHOOM
SKSHHHH
WHUNCH
CHOOM
CHOOM
CHOOM

THE ROCKET! USE THE ROCKET TO FINISH HIM!!
BUT, SIR, IF WE MISS, WE COULD DAMAGE THE--!
THEN DON'T MISS!!
WHRR
WHRR
FIRE!!
SHOOMP
CHOOM CHOOM CHOOM
BURN IN THE FIRES OF HELL, DEMON!!
FSHOOOOO
GRAAAAAH
GRA!
GRRRR...

WHAT ...?
IMPOS-
SIBLE!
WHAP

BOOM
GOTOH-SAN!!
WHRL
......
WHMM
KLA-KLAAANG
WHMM
GOTOH-SAN!!!

SBLOOOOSH
FWOOOO

SBWOOOSH
HRR—...
GOTOH... SAN...
HRR—...

—TWO YEARS PRIOR, THE EVE OF THE BUND'S OFFICIAL OPENING, THE OUTSKIRTS OF TAMA.—

HAMMER, JU-JUS' LEAVE ME...
THEY'RE CATCHIN' UP TA US... GET GOIN' WHILE YOU CAN...
SHUT UP!
TALK ANY SHIT LIKE THAT AGAIN, AND I'LL KILL YOU MYSELF!!
!

WE'VE BEEN ABAN-DONED...
LEFT FOR DEAD...

THE CAR...

!
HEH!
WELL THEN, AN ARTIFICIAL BEAST-MAN VERSUS A PACK OF THE REAL DEALS...
LET'S SEE HOW FAR I CAN GET.
DON'T, HAMMER.
RUN. PLEASE.
GRIK

VWOOOOO
GET IN!
HURRY!!

VWOOOOO
VWOOOOO
TH- THEY *DID* COME, HAMMER...
I KNEW THEY WOULD...
'M GLAD...
STUCK WITH YA...
TO THE...
...

HAMA-KUN!!
HAMA-KUN, HANG IN THERE!!
DON'T GIVE UP!
SPLASH

AUGH!!
SPLSH
WHY HIM?!
WHAT IS GOD THINKING, UP IN HEAVEN OR WHEREVER HE IS?!
WHY DOES HE HAVE TO BE THE ONLY ONE GOING THROUGH ALL THIS HELL?!

OSH
DON'T YOU *DARE* DIE ON ME, HAMA-KUN!
OOO
OOO
OOO
YOU AREN'T SOMEONE WHO DESERVES TO END THIS WAY!
YOU *HAVE* TO LIVE!
SBL
LIVE!!
WHAP
WITH ME!!

ZLLLLCH
ZLLCH
HAMA-KUN!!
SPLOSH
GOTOH... SAN...
HAMA-KUN...!
WHNG
WHNG
WHNG
BRREEEEEEE
BRREEEEEEE

I... I THINK NICOLE...
GAVE ME THAT PENDANT AS AN APOLOGY.
IT WAS HER WAY OF SAYING SORRY FOR PRE-TENDING TO BE YOU.
SHE PROBABLY MEANT FOR ME TO FIND THE MICRO-SD CARD INSIDE AND USE THE EDELMAN REPORT TO BUY MY FREEDOM FROM ROZENMANN.

BUT I DIDN'T GO BACK TO HER AFTER THAT ATTACK...
SO SHE MUST HAVE THOUGHT I'D BEEN KILLED.

HER SUICIDE BOMB ATTEMPT TO KILL MINA-HIME WAS **REVENGE** FOR WHAT SHE THOUGHT WAS MY DEATH.
IT'S MY FAULT SHE DIED.

WHAM
I DON'T HAVE ANY RIGHT TO STAY WITH YOU... I'M NOT WORTHY ENOUGH...
......
NOT AT ALL.

HEY!
OVER HERE!!

AKIRA-KUN! ELIE!!

THUK
DIE!!
DEMON!!

HAMA-KUN!
STOP THIS RIGHT NOW!
IF YOU DON'T, I'LL THROW IT INTO THE OCEAN!!
GO AHEAD!
OUR CLIENT MIGHT HAVE SOME UNPLEAS-ANT WORDS FOR ME...
BUT IT SAVES ME THE TROUBLE OF HAVING TO ALTER THE REPORT BEFORE HANDING IT OVER!

HA HA HA! LOOK AT HOW PITIFUL YOU ARE! WHERE IS YOUR VAUNTED BEASTLY STRENGTH?!
THIS IS IT!!
THIS IS WHAT I SHOULD HAVE DONE FROM THE BEGINNING!
STOP!!
GET AWAY FROM HIM!!
GOTOH-SAN, NO!
RUN...!!
ANNOYING HARLOT!
WHAP
I THINK I WILL SEND YOU TO YOUR JUSTICE FIRST!!

WATCH ME, HAMA!
IN THE END, YOU WEREN'T ABLE TO PROTECT YOUR WOMAN AFTER ALL!!
NOOOOOOO!!!
THUCK

AAARGH!
CLA-RISSA...!
WHAT ARE YOU DOING HERE?!
WHAT, DID YOU EXPECT I WOULD BE *DEAD* BY NOW?
I'M SORRY TO DISAP-POINT YOU.

WHY ARE YOU LOT JUST STANDING THERE?!
HE IS A HERETIC! DISPOSE OF HIM, RIGHT NOW!!
NO ONE WILL HEED YOUR ORDERS ANYMORE.
YOU ARE NO LONGER THE MASTER OF OUR ORGANIZATION.
WHAT?

WE HAVE LONG SINCE RETRIEVED THE EDELMAN REPORT. I HAVE READ IT.
THAT REPORT WAS ORIGINALLY CREATED BY EDELMAN AND THE PRIOR MASTER OF OUR ORGANIZATION, HIS PERSONAL FRIEND AND MY FATHER.
WHEN MY FATHER DIED UNDER MYSTERIOUS CIRCUM-STANCES, EDELMAN WAS SUSPICIOUS. HE INVESTI-GATED THE MATTER...
AND WROTE ALL OF HIS FINDINGS IN HIS REPORT!!
THE TRUTH OF YOUR PLOT TO MURDER MY FATHER AND STEAL THE COMMAND OF OUR ORGANIZATION FOR YOURSELF IS THERE FOR ALL TO READ!!

YOUR OBSESSIVE NEED TO RECOVER THE REPORT WAS NOT OUT OF ANY DEDICATION TO OUR CLIENT.
IT WAS SO THAT YOU COULD BURY ANY TRACE OF YOUR MISDEEDS!
SO WHAT?
DON'T FORGET, I WAS THE ONE TO PULL OUR ORGANIZATION OUT OF OBSCURITY AND BACK ONTO THE STAGE OF WORLD POLITICS!
I WAS THE ONE WHO BROUGHT US CONNECTIONS WITH NEW POWERS.
I WAS THE ONE WHO CONCEIVED OF OUR LARGE-SCALE PLANS, AND ACQUIRED THE MERCENARIES AND TERRORISTS TO SEE THEM THROUGH!
I WAS THE ONE WHO DID IT ALL! ME! BUT THAT STUBBORN, BLIND OLD MAN WAS SO STUCK IN THE PAST THAT HE SHUNNED ALL OF IT!!
ALL MUSTY RELICS OF THE PAST MUST BE PURGED!!
THE VAMPIRES... THE MEDIATORS...
EVEN BEASTMEN, THOSE MISTAKES OF NATURE!!
I WILL SEE THEM ALL DESTROYED BY MY OWN HAND!!

UNFORTUNATE. HAD YOU DISPLAYED ANY SHRED OF REPENTANCE...
I HAD TOLD MYSELF I WOULD FORGO EXECUTING YOU.
"EXECUTE" ME? HA!
HOW WOULD YOU DO THAT?!
DO YOU TRULY THINK YOU ARE CAPABLE OF KILLING ME?!

YES.
I ALREADY HAVE, IN FACT.

!

GAK...!
AAAGH ...!
TWITCH
TWITCH

INSTEAD OF THE BLOOD OF AGNI, I DIPPED THESE IN A FAST-ACTING POISON.
I HAVE THE ANTIDOTE RIGHT HERE, BUT I DON'T THINK YOU WILL BE NEEDING THAT ANYMORE.

THUD
LOOKS LIKE YOU'RE THE ONE WHO GETS TO START BURNING IN HELL FIRST.
HNG
HNG
DON'T WORRY. I'LL BE DOWN THERE SOMEDAY, TOO.
AND I'LL LISTEN TO ALL THE CRAP YOU HAVE TO SAY ABOUT ME THEN.
KLANG
KLANG

AREN'T YOU GONNA KILL ME?

WHEN YOU HAD THE CHANCE TO KILL ME, YOU ALLOWED ME TO LIVE.
BESIDES, BOTH OF US HAVE COMPLETED OUR OBJECTIVES. ANY FURTHER CONFLICT IS MEANINGLESS.

HN. IT SEEMS YOUR RIDE HAS ARRIVED.

BLOOOSH

BWOOO...

JIJI GAVE ME YOUR "GIFT."
THAT "EDELMAN REPORT" WAS A RATHER INTERESTING DOCUMENT.

NOW, THIS IS NOT NECESSARILY IN GRATITUDE FOR THAT...
BUT I AM SENDING YOU FROM HERE DIRECTLY TO BERGAMASQUE.
YOUR "PRIMARY CARE PHYSICIAN" IS THERE, AWAITING YOU.

THE DOC...?
YES.
YOU RESCUED HER?
IT SEEMS SHE NEVER QUIT RESEARCHING YOUR CASE.

WHILE THERE MAY BE NO WAY TO RETURN YOU TO FULL HUMANITY...
IT IS POSSIBLE TO STABILIZE YOUR TRANSFORMATIONS AND GRANT YOU A PROPER LIFESPAN. IT WILL REQUIRE A LITTLE TIME, HOWEVER.
HAMA-KUN...
HAMA!

HAMA, YOU SAVED MY LIFE. I PROMISE I'LL USE IT RIGHT AND I WON'T WASTE IT.
I'M GOING TO GROW UP INTO A WOMAN YOU CAN BE PROUD OF!

JUST LIKE REIKO.
CALL ME JO.
HUG

DO YOU REGRET COMING TO SAVE ME BACK IN AFGHANISTAN, TEN YEARS AGO?
MY WHOLE LIFE, I'VE BEEN FORCED INTO SITUATIONS WHERE MY "CHOICES" WEREN'T REALLY CHOICES AT ALL.
JOINING THE ARMY, MY DISCHARGE, THE ARTIFICIAL BEAST-MAN OPERATION, GETTING SENT TO JAPAN... NONE OF IT WAS MY CHOICE.
BUT THAT DAY...
THAT DAY, IT WAS *MY DECISION* TO RESCUE YOU. MINE ALONE.
THAT WAS THE DAY MY LIFE TRULY BEGAN.

SINCE THEN, YOU HAVE ALWAYS BEEN MY GUIDING LIGHT. THAT'S WHY I COULD NEVER TELL YOU ABOUT NICOLE.
I LIED TO YOU... I DON'T DESERVE TO BE WITH YOU AT ALL.
DO YOU REMEMBER TWO YEARS AGO?
I SAVED YOU ONCE, TOO.

DID YOU EVER WONDER WHY I WAS ANYWHERE NEAR THERE THAT DAY?
I GOT AN EMAIL. IT HAD NO SENDER, AND IT WAS UNTRACE-ABLE, BUT IT TOLD ME THAT YOU WERE IN DANGER.
NOW I KNOW THAT HAD TO HAVE BEEN FROM NICOLE.
SHE WAS THE ONE WHO BROUGHT US BACK TOGETHER AGAIN.
BOTH OF US HAVE BEEN BEATEN AND BATTERED...
AND CUT SO MANY TIMES, WE NEVER STOP BLEEDING.
BUT IF THE TWO OF US STAY TOGETHER-- HOLD ON TO EACH OTHER-- I'M SURE WE'LL BE ABLE TO STAY STANDING, NO MATTER HOW STRONG OR SHARP THE GALE.

LET ME STAY WITH YOU. PLEASE.
GOTOH-SAN...
SOME DAYS, I SWEAR...

UNCLE, LOOK.
AFTER ALL THESE YEARS...
I FINALLY FOUND IT.
YOUR ANSWER WAS RIGHT HERE.

Epilogue

YES, I HAVE JUST NOW CONFIRMED RECEIPT.
EXCELLENT WORK.
I PRAY FOR YOUR SAFE AND SPEEDY RETURN.

REJOICE, GENTLEMEN.
THE LONG SOUGHT-AFTER EDELMAN REPORT IS NOW FIRMLY IN OUR HANDS.
EXCELLENT!!

THE ONLY UNFORTUNATE NEWS IS THAT, DURING THE DOCUMENT'S RECOVERY, THE ORGANIZATION'S LEADER, MR. BOLTON, LOST HIS LIFE.
LET US ALL PRAY FOR HIS SOUL'S ASCENDANCE TO THE SIDE OF OUR HEAVENLY FATHER.
HOW TERRIBLE!
NOW WHO LEADS THAT ORGANIZATION?
I HEAR THAT MISS CLARISSA, THE DAUGHTER OF MR. BOLTON'S PREDECESSOR, HAS TAKEN THE HELM.
HER?
ER, IS THAT ACCEPTABLE? ISN'T SHE STILL QUITE YOUNG...?

WELL... MR. BOLTON WAS A PLEASANT ENOUGH FELLOW...
BUT HE HAD BECOME INCREASINGLY DEMANDING OF LATE, AND WAS PRONE TO INDEPEN-DENT ACTION.
TO BE FRANK, HE WAS BECOMING DIFFICULT TO HANDLE.
ONE OF CHINA'S MODERN HEROES SAID IT BEST, I THINK.
"IT DOESN'T MATTER IF IT IS A WHITE CAT OR BLACK; IF IT CATCHES MICE, IT IS A GOOD CAT."
THOUGH IT MAY BE IN POOR TASTE TO QUOTE ONE OF THOSE ATHEIST HEATHENS, HE HAS, ON QUICK JUDGMENT, SPOKEN AN ADMIRABLE TRUTH.
GOING FORWARD, I AM SURE WE WILL MAKE EVEN MORE PROFITABLE USE OF THAT ORGANIZATION.
BUT FOR NOW, WHAT SAY WE OPEN OUR NEWLY RECEIVED TREASURE CHEST AND ENJOY ITS SPOILS.

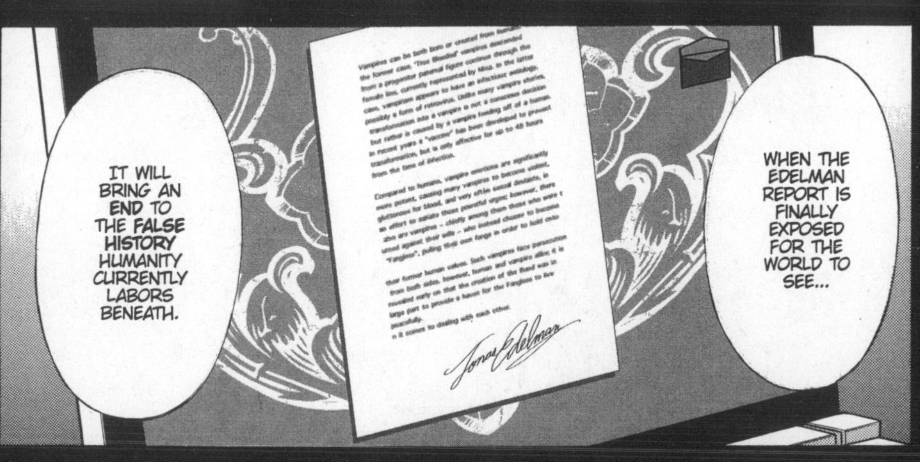
WHEN THE EDELMAN REPORT IS FINALLY EXPOSED FOR THE WORLD TO SEE...
IT WILL BRING AN END TO THE FALSE HISTORY HUMANITY CURRENTLY LABORS BENEATH.

DANCE IN THE VAMPIRE BUND: THE MEMORIES OF SLEDGEHAMMER

END